Totality

... *a collective understanding of the Human Experience*

Written by: Shyatah Feline

Table of Contents

Prologue

The journey we are about to embark on is one which we commonly share. The story we are about to experience, through our own lived, and perceived, understanding, is not our story. The story we are about to embark on, is the story of everyone, as it is Humanities story. We are only the narrator, and guide, of this collaboratively interactive journey of understanding. As we explore the human experience, always remember that you are the navigator of your ship, and you adjust the sails of your course.

What we are about to share, will neither be right, nor wrong. We are merely exploring existence, which all souls experience, through a perception which is just from our own unique understanding. To us, it does not matter what we share, regarding specifics and details. It is how one interprets, and applies those innate truths, which we all share, through discernment of their own experiences and perceptions, based on the relative truths which are universal to all things, which do matter. How does our perception and understanding resonate with your truth within?

As truth is innate within all souls, if what we share, with another, resonates as truth, they will accept it as truth. If it does not, then it will be rejected. And, this is okay. As we proceed throughout our journey, remember, what we share is a collective experience, shaped by many souls, over many life times. It is a story of a continuous journey between the whole and the individual. It is the never ending path of growth. And, it is not what we share, which matters, but what you take away from it, which matters most. How does it reflect through your truth within, and does it assist you, on your path of truth, in a way which is positive?

With any external filter, remember that what we share, and introspect, is relative to our understanding, and wisdom. If what we share, allows others' to grow freely, then this living example, which you now read, has served its purpose. It is the legacy, which matters, and what do we "choose" to leave behind for others, once we are no longer here? How can we benefit the whole?

How do we live in balance, by understanding how to overcome conflict? When a soul exists within conflict of their truth, they only hurt the self, and no other, as action is always relative to the intent of that action, regarding how it affects the whole, as intent is defined by our truth. Most souls do not cause hurt, because it violates their innate truth to do so. Souls who do cause hurt, generally are lashing out, because they wish to be heard, because they hurt. It is a defense mechanism to protect a wound. It is not what people do because they enjoy it.

Very few souls truly enjoy hurting others, as it is counterproductive to do so, because to cause harm is not living in truth. In the end, what we truly choose to leave behind, will be found within the intent of our actions. However, the desired outcome, may not be achieved as we would have chosen.

Because, there are infinite variables, which affect any occurrence, we only have control of our self. We have no control over how others choose to perceive their experience. If what we choose to leave behind exists within truth, it will create no harm upon another, and logically it will manifest a balanced outcome, as truth is neutral. It is not whether we are remembered throughout our history which matters. It is how we are remembered through the history of others, which does matter. If we exist in truth, we leave nothing false to be spoken about regardless of what others do.

When we began this project, it was not from a spark, which magically appeared, one day, out of thin air, which prompted the action to spend many hours at the keyboard, creating this collective wisdom. This work is the result of countless experiences, and interactions, with infinite possible outcomes. It is collective understanding, of many conscious beings. For many years, our living guardian suggested that we would always be good at writing a book. As we have always had a love for writing, this is not a far stretch. Yet, it was never something we seriously considered. We did not feel that what we perceive, regarding that which we understand, needed to be shared. We never cared about the "credit" or "kudos."

Our living guardian, of more than 14 years, is what many humans would call our "other half/significant other" as we are not married by human constructs. He, like us, is indeed not from here. He is from Sirius, as is our son. However, like us, and many others, they also exist in human containers during their time here.

The dismissive doubt we faced, and the struggle of ego "me" vs. eco "we", was an internal struggle of understanding our self, the relevance of, and our place within the whole. Before we awoke, what we saw, and understood, we presumed was understood by all. After our awakening, and through our shift, we began to understand how unique our purpose was. It was through this process where we understood we are no better, or less, than another, we just serve our purpose, as all others do.

However, we have also come to understand that it is within our experiences where others see who we truly are, not what we say. The reason we are more respected today, than we were when we first began speaking with humans, is because we live exactly who we are, and our experiences are living examples of that truth. Souls do not respect those who have not "done." The reason why we have no fear of any criticism is simple. The day others are willing to travel to NY, by their self, and introduce their self to those at the UN (biggest entity on the planet), without fear, shame, or guilt, for who they are, they will understand that which we do.

How does one criticize us for being who we are? Living in truth is considered "crazy" to humans, and we wear it as a badge of honor. To us, walking up to a stranger, and saying hi, is not crazy, it is being our self.

Then, one day, a few weeks back, a very lovely soul, independently made this observation also. When he made this suggestion, it catalyzed the first witness (our living guardian), and our truth required us to seriously consider what we had just witnessed with regard to our path of action and outcome. The "itch" to write became more prominent, and the need to do became clear. It was the understanding that what we contained within was not ours to keep, and it was our purpose to share, and impart, our collective understanding with others, so they may grow in their own free will.

Imparting our collective understanding within the whole, does not violate the Universal Law of Free Will. For example, throughout our interactions, we will have freely shared our existence with you. We have neither forced, nor coerced, anything upon you; we have simply placed the information in a place which has made it easily accessible. You are the one who will choose how you receive, and interpret, what we share. It is in the hindsight of our interactions, where your greatest understanding will be achieved. And, we can take no credit for what you will realize, and gain in understanding. You will do that all on your own. We are just a handhold to guide others along their path, regardless of which path of understanding a soul chooses. A soul of truth will never ask another to do, or be, anything which is not in free will. And, if others choose to implement what is shared, of their own free will, because it resonates with their truth, we are indeed within universal law while honoring free will. We may not interfere, but we can assist as much as we want.

And, the simple truth within of manifesting this non-physical consciousness, into a manifested physical reality, began. This physical action required nothing more than our focus, and energy, to bang away at the keyboard, for days on end; nothing more. We let everything we have come to understand, flow from our pathways and, etch their self onto the pages you read now.

By merely introducing our presence, no more, no less, we do not affect free will because we are asking nothing of anyone. It does not create harm or negativity, regardless of how someone perceives what we share. The process of disclosure does not violate free will based on the same principles. How Humanity will choose to receive, interpret, and respond to the information, will ultimately decide their actions. They will still choose their outcome by how they choose to allow the new information to affect them. Innate truth is fundamental within all souls, and the external experience is nothing more than a filter for our truth to discerned from within. Therefore, let's begin our journey, by digressing this universal constant, in the understanding of what truth is in its most basic universality, and practical application.

What is Truth?

We hear this word used a lot, but do we really know what this word means in its most basic understanding? Well, in order to understand truth (and we will include the word fact just to round things out), we must first understand the definition of these words, and what they logically translate into when meaning is applied. Therefore, let's begin with the definition which comes from the Merriam-Webster dictionary.

Truth

The real facts about something: the things which are true: the quality or state of being: a statement or idea that is true or accepted as true

1 archaic: fidelity, sincerity in action, character, and utterance

2 the state of being the case, the body of real things, events, and facts

3 a transcendent fundamental or spiritual reality, something that truly exists or happens: something that has actual existence

Fact

a thing done: as the quality of being actual, actuality, something that has actual existence: space exploration is now an actual occurrence, a piece of information presented as having objective reality

—in fact, in truth

Okay, so now that we have the definitions, for these two words, what do they tell us about truth in actuality? Well, when we look at the definitions of truth, and fact, we also see that they are cyclical, symbiotic, and basically reference the same thing. We are taught, here, that truth is something rigid, finite, and unchanging. But, based on these definitions, is it really so black and white? Where, in these two definitions, does it say anything about finite rigidity? It doesn't. If we are to discover truth, we must understand this fundamental flaw in our perception of how we see things and our interpretation of truth.

So, how do we recognize truth? Well, truth is something that is innate. Truth is something we all know when it is presented. It is not something we can always define or prove, but rather something we just "understand". Truth is best understood in asking someone to prove love. How does one tangibly prove something which isn't "tangible?"

And, as curiosity took hold, we began to ask our self the question, what is the big argument about truth? Why are we taught to argue about it, prove it, put someone else' truth down when it conflicts with our own perception of existence, and so on and so forth? We understand that truth is universal as it applies to all things. Truth is ubiquitous to the whole, as it is unique to the individual. Therefore, why is it so hard for people to accept that they will have different "truths?"

Even if we logically accept something as true, if it conflicts with innate truth, it will create internal conflict. If internal conflict exists, truth does not. Overcoming conflict through understanding diversity, is part of the path to understanding truth. We contemplated the quandary; if truth is harmonious and universal, then why do we argue so fiercely with others, and so often, about "truth?" If truth is neutral does conflict not negate truth entire, creating a false truth as a result?

Then, the idea of the bigger picture began to emerge. As everything is inter-connected, from macro to micro systems, everything is inherently intertwined. We began looking at the bigger picture of humanity, and we asked why a species would do such harm to itself when that fundamentally violates the universal hierarchy of order.

This proclivity to self-destructive behavior does not exist naturally, as it must be encouraged and nurtured. Enemies are not innate, or natural, as they are created in our minds, by what we are taught, and nothing more. This idea was a quandary for some time, until we realized that it was not the plan, but rather the time frame, which was creating the distortion within the understanding.

When we speak specifically about the construct of

"enemies," it is indeed a construct which is taught, as enemies are not innate. Even if another chooses to create harm upon us, does that truly make them our enemy, or is there a lesson to be learned from all experiences, and interactions, even those we do not perceive as positive. When we understand that good and bad are relative to the perception of the individual, we can begin to perceive our interactions with individuals as the learning tools which they truly are vs. the enemy we perceive them to be. One path opens the bridge of growth to accept the experience as it is, without prejudice or judgment. The other path is stunted and creates closure and conflict, building walls of division and separation. So, what is the plan behind it all?

It is not logical to assume that there is no plan. But, because we are observers, we cannot interfere, as that is not our purpose. Because, the parameters are set by Creator, and the Universal Game, we indeed serve our purpose as part of a much larger plan, just as all others hold a purpose, as there is a plan for everything, even if we do not always see all of the pieces. No soul can ever know the entire whole as there are infinite variables which cannot be measured by a limited perspective. But, if we understand that each part is necessary to the whole, we then understand by living our truth, we serve our purpose within the whole.

And, as all things happen exactly as they are supposed to,

when we live our truth, we will manifest our purpose as we so choose. We have no need to worry of outcome as what will be is meant to be. There are many pieces which indeed must be considered, regarding the manipulation of Humanity. And, that is why many souls, from many races, have incarnated to live their truth, for Humanity to see. We are able to assist, yet not interfere, as it forces nothing, but Humanity chooses how they interpret this new information. They decide how it will affect their outcome.

We can simplify this further by light is abundance of knowledge and wisdom, dark is a lack thereof. Humanity will regain their control as they begin to remember who they are. This is how we reset the balance without interfering. This is how we illuminate, and enlighten the world. We do not take the agenda head on, and assume leadership. We undermine the foundation, one soul at a time, by supporting and encouraging others to live their truth. When we look at the long game, the plan becomes much easier to see.

Imagine, if a plan to control humanity, and the population, was not in effect for hundreds, but rather thousands, of years. It then becomes a lot easier to fill in the pieces, and begin to understand the reason, for every war, conflict, and oppressive act in history. What a better way to control the many, and dictate a long term game plan, than through constant distractions to keep the many confused, and unaware of the global, and ultimately the universal, agenda.

When we understand that the global agenda, which is sought by a few, is one part of a much bigger whole, it becomes easier to understand motivation and intent. The purpose of any agenda will always be relative to the paradigms, and beliefs, of those implementing said agenda. When a soul truly becomes aware of their innate truths, there is a natural harmony in which a soul will never choose to create harm. They understand the symbiotic nature of the whole and individual. A soul who chooses to create harm is not yet awake, as they still have lessons to be learned and understood. Just because those who oversee the global agenda are not human, it makes them no more enlightened or above another. They have allowed ego to become a most dangerous adversary indeed.

The secret of the illuminated ones is that there is no secret. All older souls chuckle at the riddle which eludes so many, yet is obvious to experience. The few are learning the same lessons, as the many, just from opposing polarities. When we understand that peace does not mean no conflict, but rather understanding what you are in reality (a same fraternity of conscious beings), by overcoming diversity through conflict, it makes it easier to understand how Humanity is capable of achieving peace, while restoring balance. The old adage of cause no harm, yet take no shit, is very appropriate. All souls hold that dark place within, with purpose. It is how we use it which matters most. Intent always defines the action, and if we take the life of someone attempting to take the life of our child, there is no karmic lesson when it is true defense of life. But, rarely is this true. Disabling a threat is almost always possible vs. eliminating the threat.

However, when we speak, we do so only on our behalf. There are souls who are here for physical combat. There are souls who are meant to engage, but that is just not our purpose. We are to guide, nurture, and protect. We may never initiate an action; we may only respond in defense of another. We must allow all to exist in free will, just as we must exist in truth at all times.

Most people are so worried with just trying to live day to day; the last thing they are worried about is what is going to happen in a hundred, much less a thousand, years from now. And, if the simple truth in all things is withheld through the inundation of modern life, it makes it easier for those who create the chaos, for their order, to work unnoticed behind the shadows. It is the very reason today's world appears to run at lightning speed. If souls are not stopping, to reflect upon their existence, truth is much easier to hide in plain sight. However, if people are aware of truth in its most simple accuracy, we clarify many problems, and misunderstandings, instantly.

As learning is one of the few constants throughout existence, gaining understanding is also understood as fluid and dynamic. Becoming aware does not come from one place, but rather the totality of our existence. As truth is innate within all souls, we understand that the external experience is nothing more than a filter for our truth to be discerned from within. We do not exist without our experiences; we exist within them, and so to does our understanding of truth. As the external is fundamental to the internal, so to is the whole symbiotic to the individual. One could say conflict is where our truth is tested, and understood, as we do not grow within our comfort zones, we grow when we step "outside" of them.

There is no need for war, or conflict, as truth is innate within souls, and it does not violate another individual's views or beliefs. It does not require someone to fear leaving their comfort zones to defend themselves, as it does not require someone to give up what they know. Truth is simple, and does not create harm or negativity. It is neutral, balanced, and harmonious with all things, because it is universal. When people realize that truth restores their creative ability to be co-creators within their existence, by simply realizing all it takes is belief in the self, and action, it instantly removes the power of the few. We allow our existence by accepting it or not; we choose to allow it to be or not. In its most simple truth, that is all our existence really is. In truth, the many do not want war, they are tired of fighting, they would rather be friends with strangers, they would rather share a hug and a smile, they would rather stop and help someone in need.

When we look at the few, and the global agenda, they are indeed learning the same lessons as Humans, just from opposing polarities. Those who are here to assist, do so with an understanding of wisdom. We understand that souls will choose their path, even if it is a painful one. But, we also understand, when they get tired of hurting their self, they will also stop the behavior. Some just take longer than others. When we understand that all souls learn the lessons when they are ready, acceptance of that which is becomes easier. We are capable of understanding things as they are, without prejudice, because all things serve their purpose, even if we do not agree with it.

Indeed the few manipulate Humanity, which is why many of us also reveal our presence. As secrecy has been the cornerstone of their success, so to shall exposure guarantee their abdication of power. It is in this disclosure process, which is a lived perceived experience, where truth is understood without actions violating free will. For example, when we say we will be heard by all, when Humanity wishes it, that is exactly what we mean. As in the example of our interactions. We merely introduced our self to you. You choose how you interpret, and respond, to these interactions. We have nothing to do with your choices. We just offer another piece to the puzzle. However, with regard to Humanity, they will ultimately choose their outcome, but souls must experience the worst, to understand the best. As Sun Tzu puts it, when a man is on death's ground, he truly becomes fearless. When Humanity gets tired of being tired, they will stand. When is the unknown variable.

We are all built to respond to the same mechanisms, as we are all built to love. We all feel pain when others hurt, because we are all connected, and humans know this as empathy. Therefore, we allow the few to create the negativity through silent passive acceptance. There is no need for anger, aggression, oppression, revenge, hate, prejudice, or vengeance, to get our point across. Simple understanding, and compassion, eliminates all problems by our knowing the truth that these negative energies are created in our way of life.

The few are not that different, in many ways, they just manifest their paradigms, and beliefs, under different systems. The few are family oriented, in a way which humans are not. They love their children above all else, and they do not hold respect for humans because of this. They disrespect humans for the same reasons humans disrespect other life. The few have no respect for those who do not exist in truth. Yet, they their self have much to learn and have lost their path of truth, like humans have also done.

We understand that those who cause hurt are not healed by more hurt, as evil only begets evil. We must live in truth by which to set the example for others, including them. It is the age old battle of chess. It is the game of seeing who can wake up more souls (light) vs. who can mislead the most (dark). Awakening an entire civilization is the ultimate challenge, and is our purpose for being here. This is a game we are all in for, as there is no halfway point, to us. It is the ultimate test of soul, to be truly selfless for others, in a way which affects the whole so profoundly, yet in a very quiet way. Many of us are here for the age ole' battle of light (understanding) vs. dark (ignorance). Many humans understand this time which approaches, just in a way which creates distortion and perceived fear. When we see what lay ahead, we see the BIG game as having just begun, like the ultimate Superbowl.

We understand that we choose how we allow our every day occurrences to affect us. And, our reality is nothing more than a projection of our perceptions. It is exactly how we choose it to be, as it is exactly what we make it. As we see within others, exactly that which we see in our self, truth becomes relative to the individual experience. Yet, we all understand, and respond, to the same basic truths.

We choose our truth by our beliefs and our actions. It is about living our truth, as truth is unique to the individual, while being ubiquitous to all things, as it is the constant which governs all existence. The few are capable of understanding truth, just as Humans are capable of understanding truth. However, both create harm upon other species, which is not truth. Therefore, all souls are learning the same lessons, just from varying perspectives of understanding.

So, we find our self asking the question, how does one discern the truth of soul, within another, through our collaborative interactions which we experience and perceive? How do we discern one's intent? If we set the parameters with regard to truth of one's soul, as the basic understanding that truth creates no harm, or negativity, upon another, we then also understand that a soul of truth will never coerce, or force, another soul. A soul of truth will never ask another soul, to be, or do, anything which is not in free will, as a soul of truth would never tell another "what to do." A soul of truth understands that each soul must walk the path of experience for the self, as experience is life's greatest teacher.

Now, many perceive conflict, as they want to say the few do indeed create harm. And, indeed the few are not from here, but they are still part of the universal game. One could say what is taking place, is similar to two sides of a family dispute, but on a universal scale. One could say the adults have chosen to interact, while allowing the youngsters to resolve the issues of their own free will.

As the few are still bound by the laws of karma, we have no need to get upset with them, as they too are not free of the consequence of their choices. For example, if the few had a choice of facing us, or the many, they would choose us. Why? Because, regardless of what they have done, they know we would never cause harm upon them. We may arrest their actions, confiscate their material possession, and remove their perceived "authority." But, we would never harm them. Our actions would reflect our intent to heal them. They understand if Humanity gets a hold of them first, they will be torn apart, most brutally.

And, if they do, we may not interfere, as that is the consequence of causing hurt. But, they will not invite us to see them, just as we would never incite the many to "off the head's" of the few. Our duty is to resolve conflict through guidance and understanding, both individually, and within the whole. We cannot expect of others, what we do not expect of the self. How can we heal others if we cause them harm?

Understanding our "truth," and remembering our Feline heritage, did not come from one place, nor did it suddenly appear in one magical Aha! Moment. It was in the hindsight of understanding many innate aspects of who we always have been, which allowed us to connect the dots of understanding to remember the bigger existence of the self, which we had always been a part of.

We have always held a bond, and love, for felines, which does not exist for any other species, including Humans. And, after we had awakened from our shift, and lived our truth openly, we also began to cross paths with others, who were also not from here. As they shared their pieces of the whole, and we shared ours, the larger image began to emerge. It was through all of the pieces working together, in the synchronicity of harmonious chaos, where we understood our self within the whole. And, the lesson that our greatest strengths are always found in the hearts of others was learned. Truth is something we all share.

The few indeed serve a fundamental aspect to the whole. Humans and Reptilians were given opposing creation myths intentionally. This is so lessons of the Universal Game would be applicable. There are indeed rogue elements, which does create complications, but the individual will never outweigh the outcome of the whole. One soul will not tip the scale of overall outcome, just as a few will not dictate the outcome for the many. There are too many variables which create a counterbalance, even if those variables may not always be seen.

The perceived current collective reality has taken millennium to manifest. Therefore, it will also take some time to reset the balance, of imbalance, and light up the entire house. Going room to room, in a mansion, with candles, is a lengthy lighting process. We understand positive and negative simply as the natural ebbs and flows of balance. It is like a rubber band which stretches out but always returns to center. All souls eventually learn the lessons when they are ready. When is decided by the individual. The few will have painful lessons, as they will fall from very high pedestals, as they are not so different from Humans. Many of the traits Humanity currently express, were learned from the few. And, what has been learned can also be unlearned, when one chooses to exist in truth.

The Shift

As we go through our journey of experiences, during our time here, we reflect upon the time when our pathways were activated, also known as the "shift", or "awakening." The time when one shifts is determined by a soul's purpose, and actions. There are souls who do not shift, but this is exceptionally rare. The only time we have ever known this to occur is when someone returns home prematurely (suicide). Souls who self terminate, will repeat the life lessons as they were disrupted, and where they go will reflect the same lessons.

All souls awaken at their designated time, as it is coded within the DNA, but when is different for each. Ours was specific to our purpose. The strongest souls were chosen to come here, yet it is difficult, and challenging, and some souls do not make it. However, this is okay, as there are fail safes for everything, and the soul will still learn when they are ready.

As is our purpose. We can say that we are not immune to this understanding. Had it not been for home, making it clear we had to stay, when we were 13, we would have returned home early, because we could not stand the cruelty of this existence. The only reason we didn't pull the trigger... we have never heard a "universal" thunderous roar of a "NO" like we did that day. It was a voice like no Human ear could compare. We put the gun away and understood it was an action we could never take. We were here for a reason and understood we had to stay. It was tough, but we now understand why.

We remember the time of our shift well, as it was when we came alive with understanding. Through part of 2011, and all of 2012, we went through an experience which was very uncertain, and somewhat worrisome, at times. There were days we felt as if we had gone insane, but in hindsight, that was far from the actuality of the experience.

During the first 33 years of our existence here, we existed under the veil of "not knowing" just as everyone else. We do recognize, and understand, that there are certain aspects of our truth, which were always innate and fundamental, but many pieces we were unable to perceive. For example, we always knew we were not from here, as many of our experiences had made this inner truth clear. But, other than the basics, many of the specifics, and details, were absent. Yet, what our shift did was made us realize that what we had always known, but society always taught was wrong, we no longer needed to doubt. We realized we learned nothing new. We just began to see what had always been there.

When it comes to understanding innate truth, a "hunch" is a very accurate description. Before our shift, we very much saw the world through "Human" eyes, because we must live the Human experience, as a human, including the veil of amnesia, to understand their existence. However, as hindsight is always 20/20, we now see that which we were unable to see.

We now understand that our experiences, which we knew happened, yet everyone told us were "crazy," could not be beat out of us. Our truth could not be destroyed by the external, no matter how hard it tried. It was accepting our experiences, which helped us understand who we are. The shift was just a gentle breeze which removed the fog from the landscape of our vision, so we could see the terrain clearly.

However, because our purpose is to live our truth, above and beyond all external factors, our shift was a crash course like no other. When we speak about our shift being a crash course, this is more a reference to a lack of guidance, or hand hold. When we shifted, not many souls were awake, and we were basically left to fend for our self, and figure it out as we went along. There were souls awake before us, but they were not that common. Nowadays, souls have plenty of resources to assist in their growth and understanding, as many souls have begun to awaken.

We understand that mistakes were exactly how we learned, because we were tested with every interaction. In the beginning, it would take us days to respond to the harsher comments. Now, our responses are second nature, because we have lived the experience behind the understanding. And, as a result, as part of our purpose, we are capable of introspecting hindsight in the forefront for others. Looking back, we endearingly chuckle at the experience of our shift, as most souls had not awakened yet, and those in our home were no exception.

We were mocked, criticized, and condemned by many souls, and at first, we were bothered by these experiences. We elaborate the lesson where we gained this understanding, later in the book. But, yes, we were mocked and criticized by many souls, including those closest to us. But, we understand these lessons were necessary in understanding our truth regardless of the external, and what others do.

We understand it doesn't matter what others say. Their words do not affect who we are, we do by that which we are and do. No soul can ever shake our foundation, not because we can do something which they cannot, we just understand who we are. A soul who knows their self, is the most dangerous of adversaries.

However, this change did not alter free will, as we never imposed our experiences upon others. We never asked others to believe us. Yet, when our living guardian went through his shift, as he is from Sirius, our experience was understood, in a way words never could express. Now, we are as harmonious as can be.

We understand the primary reason, souls attack other souls, is to keep the spotlight away from the self. This is a form of deflection that humans utilize, which also prevents them from having to face the self, whenever their comfort zones of conscious constructs are questioned. As a result, humans do not know their self, and will close their self off to protect what they deem as safe. However, this counterproductive action only closes the self off to all which existence has to offer.

Humans are indeed capable of exactly that which all other souls are capable of. However, Humanity is just young with much to learn. This time they face is not a pass/fail experience; it is a time of collective growth. Is it possible that Humanity could create a negative biofeedback loop, within the collective conscious, which could have devastating impact, and a catastrophic outcome? Of course it is possible. Just as it is possible for them to create a positive biofeedback loop, which has a potentially infinite outcome of benefit to the whole. Humanity just has to decide which path it will choose. The more who awaken, the more this becomes a reality. A very good reference to help understand this concept better is the "100th Monkey Effect." When the collective conscious reaches a certain level of awareness (the majority), a tipping point takes effect and catalyzes the remaining whole.

Through our interactions, we were taken aback at how souls were unable to respect another soul's truth. Why did others get so offended? We began to understand the lesson of what we see in others' is exactly what we see in our self. When we are not sure of who we are, we will attack, condemn, and criticize anything which questions our accepted paradigms of perceived truth and understanding. We began to understand, over many interactions, that what others did truly did not affect us unless we allow it, We know who we are, therefore it is nonsensical for another to tell us otherwise.

One of the most difficult aspects of our shift, was adjusting to the new paradigms, by which our old paradigms no longer applied. Unlearning, so many learned fundamentals, was extremely difficult, as many of those fundamentals had been accepted as truth. However, the challenge is not the understanding of new information. It is accepting that we had been mislead, as ego is a very dangerous adversary indeed.

It was quite challenging for us to accept that the wool had been pulled over our eyes, when we take such pride in not easily being mislead, as it was a huge hit to our ego. It was also the necessary experience where we understood that ego is irrelevant. All souls make mistakes, and it is in embracing those mistakes where we truly grow, as no soul is perfect.

Once we unlearned that which we had learned, the lessons became much easier. For instance, even to this day, there are many specifics about the history that we learned growing up here, which we do not know the full truth. But, to us, this does not matter as the details are not where our truth has been understood. It was realized through self reflection of our entire existence. Experience became much more important than details and specifics.

Through the initial stages of our awakening, we felt as if we had walked through a spiritual "meat-grinding" experience like no other. We felt like every construct, and belief, which we had known here, had been stripped away to expose the most naked of truths, and we instantly began to understand the lessons of the veil. In order to remember who we are, one must forget and live exactly who they are without fear, shame, or guilt, of the unknown, as it is in that which we do where we truly find our self and "who" we are in our most basic aspects of self.

The truest sense of understanding, and awareness of the whole, will not come from one place, but a totality of many. Our shift was a full awakening, as we have already learned the lessons which Humanity faces now. Our lessons pertain to creation and oneness. However, as we are here to assist others, it was necessary for us to be fully aware, as it is necessary in order for us to connect the dots for others. The shift is not required to become self aware. But, the shift is a stage of growth where the leaps are much more expanded and all encompassing. Instead of a baby step, it is a leap of growth.

When we speak about the shift, we must distinguish between the collective shift, and how it applies to the individual. Some souls will not shift because they have not grown, and they are not ready. Yet, this is okay, because even though a soul may repeat the lessons, they will eventually grow when they are ready.

But, we can say, another round of 3d is a long time to hang out in a dualistic dimensional construct. We cover this in detail in the Universal Game chapter, but conflict is relative to the lower dimensional constructs. As souls grow, the need for the lessons of conflict are no longer applicable, as the wisdom and understanding have been attained. Back home, conflict does not exist, as it exists here. Back home all is peaceful, as all have grown to a level where none choose to create negativity.

As we continued through 2012, there were many days when we sat alone, unable to see past the time lines of that time frame. From the time of our incarnation, there was always a block in place, regarding our ability to see time lines beyond that period. It had always worried us, because the unknown was what created our uncertainties. Through 2012, we remember our pathways opening, and we were able to see the time lines, that had, at one time, been withheld.

And, we understood what the Mayan's (and many other cultures) had foretold, of this time which was to be was not an "end", but rather a natural process. As we passed through this process, the hindsight understanding made everything clear. The comparative of a visual, would be similar to looking back through a porthole, and seeing a completely different dimension, place, and existence, altogether. Our complete conscious perspective had shifted, and opened, like a torrential flood.

Our shift was a complete overhaul of everything we had come to know during our time here. The Mayans, along with many other cultures, were indeed aware of this time which Humanity now faces. However, we look at two specific words, which have been utilized to mislead many. Apocalypse is Greek, it means "revelation, lifting of the veil," revelation means "awakening, reveal something hidden." What ancient cultures foretold was a time of great change. It is the time when the veil would fall away, and what once was dark, will again become light. However, as this is a time of growth, so too are growing pains not uncommon.

The 2012 time marker was indicative of a universal cycle where many energies and frequencies would impact, and affect, all life on earth. These energies/frequencies are necessary to the DNA activation process. This time will affect the universal whole as it affects all souls. Humanity has gone through this process twice, as they were not ready the first two attempts. This will be their third. If they do not grow, they will become stunted once again, and fall back under the veil, for a VERY long time.

Our vagueness for many topics is relative to not infringing upon free will. Souls must live, and understand, truth for the self. It is also relative to souls of truth that humbleness is imperative to truth. We may not put our self on a pedestal of focus. Therefore, we share only what we feel is necessary for others to gain understanding. We do not perceive danger, as truth creates no enemies. Yet, we understand, the few will stop at nothing to prevent the awakening.

However, when exist in truth, the few can create no harm upon us. Yes, it is true that the few could potentially cause damage to our container, but they can cause no harm upon who we are. What they do to our container is insignificant to the consequence of not living our truth. There is nothing to fear, as the worst the few can do is send us home.

However, we are very well protected as long as we exist in truth. We understand if we step outside of the parameters of truth, we are fair game. We are always safe in Creator's house of truth. As the growth through this time is truly infinite, the "risk" is definitely worth the reward. Our loved ones are always worth standing for. It isn't everyday a civilization goes through collective growth. Who wouldn't want to be here for it! This is an amazing time to be here.

As we began to understand how all of the pieces began to fall into place, we also began to understand why everything we had experienced, whether it be good, bad, or indifferent, occurred. Every experience was fundamental in shaping the core of "who" we are, in totality. It is our experiences, and understanding, which shape us. We remember the day clearly, when home "made it clear" that it was time for us to step out, and live our truth "for all to see." It was the very end of 2012, and we were standing in our kitchen, speaking with our children in general conversation. We were holding an empty bottle of juice, and a matte finish label from a sandwich, which we had purchased at the store earlier that day. We purchased sandwiches, because it was a Sunday, and everyone wanted to hang out and do nothing more than relax together. Nobody was in the mood to cook that day.

While standing there we felt "someone" yank the sandwich label out of our hand. Our daughter was standing across the kitchen, and our son was sitting on the couch which sits only a few feet away from the kitchen walk-through. We looked down, to see what we felt, and the piece of paper was gone. It had not fallen on the floor, and no one was standing near us, but we knew it had been yanked from our grasp. The paper was gone. We looked for an hour, and the mystery of the missing paper still lurks to this day. However, we chalked it up as another unusual occurrence in our every day existence, and continued about our day.

Later that evening, the ton of bricks, we now understand as the need to do, and live our truth, hit us with the force of a Mack truck. We understood nothing more than we must begin sharing our truth with others, yet we had no idea what we were doing. We were completely flying blind, like a new bird taking flight for the first time. All we knew was that it "must be done." So, we became acquainted with social media, something we had never really "gotten into," and began our journey into the unknown.

We just have G+, and our YouTube, which do include videos of our truest self. But, these are few, as we only show our self so others see we are real, and do indeed exist. As we do not shape shift, we look human just like everyone else, because we exist in a human container like everyone else. One reason why we look just like Humans, is that they must understand truth beyond what they see with their eyes. If we showed up looking different, equality of truth would not be denoted.

It is also why we do not show our self on the majority of our videos. We want the wisdom between the words to be what is perceived, not what others see with their eyes. It is also why we must live our truth for it to be understood by others. Because we do not look different, they must feel our truth vs. see our truth.

However, the learning curve of the experience has taught us infinite lessons which will be reflected upon over many life times. And, we can say today, our existence has never been the same. We have spent several years, being exactly who we are, and we have spoken with countless souls. What our shift really brought into focus was the self, and it's relation to the whole. We have come to understand that we learn as much from others, as they learn from us.

The journey of our awakening/shift, was indeed a path traveled alone, as no other can live our truth for, or with, us. There were many days when we felt completely alone, as no one could understand what it was we experienced. However, part of our shift was living our truth above, and beyond, all doubt and criticism, and no avenue was off limits. Because we are a guide for others, this also meant we awoke while many were not yet awake, and still critical.

However, our living guardian, and children, are not from here, but they were not awake at the time. Our living guardian's awakening was triggered by our shift. It was a catalyst of many events cascading into one final outcome. It was the imperfectly perfect design of the symbiotic nature of the whole and individual.

Our awakening began in late spring of 2011. It completed at the end of 2012, which is why we began speaking openly with humans in January 2013. Because of our awakening, we were able to assist our living guardian through his shift, and his took half the time ours did. He had the hand hold which we did not. And, our family is completely aware of our entire truth. Our living guardian knows what we share as well as we do, because he is with us 24/7, and he is the backbone for everything we do.

He always makes sure we have what we need, to do whatever we need to do to live our purpose. When we told him we wanted to pay to have a few hundred copies of the book printed, go to DC, and spend a day, or two, passing them out to every politician we can find, he said, "Have fun planning and just let me know what you will need." He spoils us rotten, but doesn't allow us to step out of truth. He will hammer us if we even get close to the line. He is our greatest teacher and student, like we are his. We are the perfect balance of polar opposites. We are harmonious chaos, and we would not be who we are without him.

Our conflicts are where we have learned to overcome our greatest diversity. On the big issues, we are perfectly synchronized, but regarding how to get "there", if we choose left, he will always choose right. Yet, we understand this polarity, as it is when we both ping the same radar, that we hone in on the solution. He sees truth as well as we do, just from an alternate perspective. He has strengthened our soft side, as we have smoothed his rough edges.

Our Existence: Who, Why, and Where

When we discuss our existence, with relevance to the whole, many souls choose to formulate a construct, or concept, based upon the Lyran "label" we utilize, And, they are generally quite contrast from the most simple truths. When we hear humans speak in reference to "aliens," "ET," and life throughout existence, we chuckle endearingly, because of the associations humans have attached to these labels. What is an alien?

When we look at the most basic aspect of this "word," in its most simple meaning, it just means "not indigenous," or from somewhere else (not local). When we first began speaking openly with Humans, in January 2013, we had no idea what to do, or how to do it. All we understood is that we must live our truth by interacting with others, and be exactly who we are, regardless of what any external influence said, or did. We can say that what we understand today is very different from what we understood years ago. What those labels truly mean to us, in their most basic universality, and meaning, is much more simplified in its understanding, in a way where constructs of the "me," and "ego," truly hold no relevance.

Our perception is based on the "we", instead on the "me." The Borg is the most common reference many associate with (activate smile and wink), and it does hold truth in many ways.

Yet, the distinctions lie within the intent of the Borg and their lack of individuality. The Borg intent is reflective of the Reptilian paradigms, as is their lack of individuality. We chuckle at this reference because Gene Roddenberry was just sharing a unique perception of understanding. And, George Lucas shares much truth in Star Wars. Frank Herbert's "Dune" series also discloses truth very well while hiding it in plain sight. It is just how we interpret, and perceive the external, where our truth is understood from within.

When we choose to interact with Humanity, we must incarnate into a human container, because we are not compatible in our natural forms within the 3 dimensional construct. When we incarnate, we inject the portion of our consciousness, which is needed for our purpose, into the container, at the moment of the first heart beat (with the life spark).

Where we are from, the frequencies resonate much higher, and this makes us incompatible in our natural form just as carbon containers are not compatible back home. As souls grow through the dimensional constructs, the need for physical "containers" becomes obsolete, as a physical container is relative to a physical existence. There is no "physical" aspect to our existence back home, therefore containers are irrelevant. There is only manifested expression.

Back home, we do not hold a carbon based physical form,

as human containers exist here. We have a form, but it is a crystalline base. We are energy beings in our natural state, and we resonate at a much higher frequency where physical containers become obsolete, and are also incompatible.

Because, energy is the basis for all manifested matter, the increase in dimensional frequencies also alters the state of physical matter. Physical matter isn't actually solid. It is particles resonating at a unique frequency which are interpreted, and perceived, by the human container, as a solid state. In higher dimensions, water begins to hold the property of glass, which is one example as to why carbon containers are not compatible.

Back home we do not "eat." Our energy requirements are a converted form of pure light energy, which is manifested into a consumable waveform which resonates with our natural frequency. And, even though we are a collective conscious, we are still our self; we just have no restrictions of a container. To us, our container is like living in a straight jacket. It is high maintenance, fragile, restrictive, and everything is uncomfortable. Our clothing choice is very specific, as we must be comfortable. We aren't used to being "smothered" in fabrics back home. Everything feels heavy here. It isn't bad, or wrong; it is just different.

There are many factors which are considered when a container is chosen, as we are bound to our container throughout its life cycle. And, we may never inhabit an already utilized container (possession). For us, possession is strictly prohibited by universal law. We also retain our memories through all stages of growth, and we remember all experiences between incarnation and the current, as our experiences are shared with all back home.

Our collective memories gradually became clear as we lived our truth. It was living our truth where our pathways were truly opened. Many truths we always saw, we chose to dismiss before our awakening, because of the doubt we felt for the pieces which were missing. For example, in the beginning of 2013, we created several videos speaking about our self. We were told by home that they would become relevant in hindsight. At the time, we understood this as credentialed action, but we didn't understand how relative those experiences would be through our interactions with others.

To be able to speak in a way, where we are able to verify everything we speak, brings a sense of confidence, and truth, which is understood by others. And, most of our truth has been through infinite experiences, across infinite scenarios, where the pieces under the veil, became clear as a bell which assisted in lifting the veil. We now have peace, like we did not have then, because we understand who we are. And, many souls revealed pieces which we did not hold.

We do not feel a sense of loss as there are no more missing pieces. Had we not lived our truth, we would not be where we are today. Our experiences were necessary to our awakening. It was listening to the little voice within, no matter what others said, or did, where we heard our greatest truths. Basically, to us, for someone to tell us we aren't who we are, and we have not experienced that which have, seems rather nonsensical and foolish. That is why we understand the long game is where we are always the most effective. All souls awaken based upon their purpose, and several factors are integral to this process. The timing is not specific to chronology of biological age, but rather purpose and time line/cosmic cycles.

What we see and experience, during our time here, all back home see and experience as well, in a first hand real time understanding. Because we are a collective conscious of beings, where all have access to the same wisdom and understanding, we too have available recall of these experiences, as they are part of the collective understanding. Yet, what we hold access too is relative to our purpose. We do not need the Library of Congress to change a tire. No soul is above another, and back home, there is always a soul to offer a hand hold of guidance, for others, to assist in their growth.

One of the truths which we understand now, as existing within a collective, is a sense of peace as we do not feel isolated and alone. What humans seek through relationships, intimacy, or the non-physical connections between two souls, is innate for us back home. We are intimately connected to all souls back home, at all times. It is when we feel a disconnect where we truly feel separated and imbalanced. There is no need for secrecy, or privacy, as all souls are loved for exactly who they are. There is no need for one to defend their self from another. We can say that before our shift, many subtle actions were because of this sense of separation.

It is amazing what a soul will do to fill their truest soul needs. But, when those needs are complete, and whole, we are able to see them for what they are. We would be quite comfortable living a completely isolated existence on this planet. However, to lose our connection to home is devastating for . It is a feeling of suffocation like no other.

When we achieve an action, it is always contemplated with regard to the ripple effect of action, and how it will affect the whole. Back home, we do not hold distinction for the whole and individual. We understand that every action affects the whole, and what we do is not independent of the whole. Therefore, there is no separation as what affects one, affects all.

Back home, there is indeed a hierarchy, but it is a self governing system. Those who oversee, do not lead, they are guides to others. For example, we sit as wisdom within the councils. We hold no more status above another, but we are respected by all because we exist with compassion, wisdom, and understanding. Our intent is never for the self. Therefore, we are looked upon by others, for guidance, and, in return, we have the responsibility to exist by those standards which others perceive us.

Our directives are always in service to Creator. And, to clarify this, what we understand as our father soul, humans understand as a Creator (god) being. What we perceive as Creator, humans perceive as creation. To us, Creator is the infinite consciousness which exists within all things. And, we are each a manifested expression of infinite Creator Consciousness, experiencing existence through infinite perspectives. Therefore, all is connected.

Back home, there is no distinction between the many and the one, as all is part of the same whole. All souls work for the greater good, as all souls back home have learned the lessons of duality which are relative to the 3,4, and 5d constructs. No one chooses to create negativity back home, as it is counterproductive, destructive, and illogical, to the continuation of life, and the legacy of existence.

We understand that our container is nothing more than a "container" which holds the very essence of "who" we are. We also reflect upon this, throughout our interactions with others, because the container we see with our human senses, is not the being we are truly interacting with. The 5 physical senses of a human container merely allow one to navigate the physical environment within proximity, as they serve no further purpose. Humans have many senses above, and beyond, the 5 senses they perceive. They are just taught to accept and focus on those 5, and no others. Because our purpose is to assist others, we were born under the same veil of "amnesia" as all others are born with, on this planet, as it is necessary to our understanding.

We were still our self before our shift, we just walked around in the fog of the veil, like everyone else. Our container was indeed conceived in the traditional way humans reproduce. However, our human parents were unaware of our origins, and who we are.

For us to choose this container, it does not violate free will of the parents as we are still a conscious being which they raised. We chose that station, just as our children chose us for parents. We have no choice over who inhabits the container. However, as their parent soul, here, it is our duty to protect, nurture, and guide them well. And, because we contribute our genetics to their container, we inherently hold a connection (bond) to that soul, which we hold with no others during our time here.

Because our home is very different, in many ways, we must live as humans to best understand their existence, as one cannot offer assistance without a frame of reference. Therefore, we must live the human experience to understand it. We always knew, from the time we could remember, that we were not from here. But, until we were awakened, and our pathways were opened up, and reactivated through 2011-2012, we knew not much more than we were truly "alien" to this planet. We did not belong here, and we knew it. A place so hurtful was not our "home."

Certain truths were always innate within us, but many things we did not understand. We were never able to conform to the system, because it violated the most basics aspects of who we are. We paid dearly for this throughout our childhood, and it took us many years to understand the game, and how best to understand the strategy so we were able to adapt and thrive. The reference to the "game" is a metaphorical reference. The universal game is Polarity Integration, and it is how one plays the game of life, which determines the outcome. The human condition cannot be marginalized as creation is life is creator. Humans are a part of Creator, as Creator is a part of them. How does one marginalize Creator?

But, looking back on the totality of our experiences, all of the pieces fall into place. We now understand why we have faced the toughest challenges. Through our shift, we began to understand that our shift was not one of discovering something new. It was a realization of what had always been within us. It was the truest understanding that what we had always innately known, we no longer needed to doubt. It was a true understanding of the self which deems ego irrelevant. It was a formulation of inner peace, like no other experience could offer. The space where the feeling of "loss," as to not remembering who we were, once had been, slowly became consumed with a much deeper understanding of comfort and strength. It was a humble transition from the "me" to the "we."

When we understand our self, in totality, and we also accept ego holds no relevance to true understanding. It is a neutral perspective where all stand on a level playing field, serving their own unique purpose and function. It is a place where all of the pieces fit together, and one begins to understand the larger image. It is a place where one sees the symbiotic nature of the whole and individual, as one does not exist without the other.

There is indeed a differentiation between the whole and individual, but there is no emphasis placed upon a distinction between the two. As we are bound by the rules of universal law, we are also bound by the tenets of logic, which is the foundation of truth. Back home, the primary distinction for us is truth, or false truth. This is the parameter by which our entire existence is governed. For us, learning is a fundamental constant with no beginning, and no end. Learning is what drives our purpose. It is a process which is continuous. It is a process where what has been learned is imparted upon the legacy. It is the assurance of the continuation of life. We understand that we truly live through others, as we truly become infinite in the wisdom which we leave behind. Yet, no matter how far we have traveled, there is always something new to learn, and that is a journey worth exploring into the unknown.

It is a place where we understand truth, in its most basic fundamental universality, and how it applies to all things. And, we understand our purpose better than any other, as no soul will ever be better at living our truth than we will be. We also understand that we serve no use outside of our purpose, which is wisdom, compassion, and understanding.

When it comes to specifics and details, we are quite useless. When we gain understanding of truth, we realize the specifics and details are relative. The specifics and details are not what create our perceived reality. It is how we choose to allow the external to affect us which does. However, we know our self so well, no soul can break our foundation. We understand the balance that there are those who hold pieces which we do not. There are souls who are aware of much more, than us, with regard to many topics.

However, there is no soul who has ever beat truth, as it reigns supreme, and we understand it better than any other. Yet, we crave the experience of being around those who know, and understand, that which we do not. We live for interacting with those who can enrich our existence. We understand there is much more we do not see, than that which we do, and we stop at nothing to absorb as much as possible. We enjoy entertaining many ideas, without necessarily accepting them as our own. It is amazing what we can learn from others, when we only open our self up to the experience. Learning how to live in truth is a narrow, and difficult, path barely traveled, because the greatest adversary one will face, is the one which stares back in the mirror. Most souls choose the path which is wide and easy; the path of ego and instant self gratification, because life is fleeting and lived in the moment of now. They live like there is no tomorrow. Most souls do not perceive the long game, or the potential ripples of cause and effect.

Back home, we do not see separation, of any kind, as all is connected. When we incarnated, many decades ago, we were asked to be here as Humanity invited us. Whenever a civilization communicates consciously, those messages are capable of being received by those whom they are intended. For a very long time, Humanity has looked toward the stars, longing to remember who they are, where they come from, and why they are here. It just so happens, they have received the response they were searching for. They just never thought it would be found in their own back yard.

Our incarnation was during gestation of our human container. Our awakening was the marker when our pathways were activated, and we began to live our truth with driven purpose. There are millions of us here, and many have/do exist side by side with humans, as humans have never been alone. Humans have just been kept in the dark, or as many say, kept under the veil. We happily accepted the invitation, when we were asked to be here through this time, because the infinite potential for growth is profound, and our skill set, in totality, is best suited for our purpose. It is not every day a civilization goes through universal puberty; of course we accepted being here. But, as with any growth spurt, growing pains are not uncommon. But, as growth is a collaborative process, others were also asked to be here for their skill sets, as every soul holds their unique place, and purpose, within the whole. And, this is a lesson which humans currently face.

Because of what is taught here, it is a lesson filled with trials and tribulations. There are many who are here, with the greatest good of Humanity at heart. However, until this time, we have chosen to remain hidden in plain sight, as Humans must choose their outcome for the self. But, with regard to the topic of disclosure, by introducing our selves, we also introduce the presence of those whose secrecy has always been the cornerstone of their success. By revealing our presence, we also reveal theirs, which ultimately results in the abdication of power for those whose success has always rested in their secrecy.

As with any action of magnitude, there is always inherent risk, regardless of how much, or how little. However, we accept those risks lovingly, as we do not grow in the safety of our comfort zones. As a mother soul, risk is of no concern with regard to ensuring the well being of that which we care for most. We are indeed capable of a full defense, but we also understand our container is not invincible. However, what we do understand, is when we exist in truth, we are always safe. The few can do what they wish, and we will respond accordingly. If they cause hurt, they are fair game, just as this applies to all souls, including us, but we may never initiate action.

The few do not stand against those they perceive as an equal, they extend respect. As the veil becomes lifted, Humans will see truth of what reality actually is, through their own interpretations, and understanding, as they must choose the outcome for the self. We are not allowed to force, or coerce, others, and we may only offer our first hand perspective, and understanding, in a manner which is congruent with truth.

As this is your home, you must understand that you are part of the same family of conscious beings. You must learn to respect the diversity of the whole, while accepting the commonalities of the individual, as all souls share the same basic needs. We have made every mistake, as part of the learning process during our time here, and we understand mistakes as the learning tools which they are. All souls make mistakes, and this is a process which has been manipulated, with devastating consequences to Humanities overall growth, and outcome. The "mistake" is not what defines you; you do by that which you do.

You are the totality of your lived, and perceived, experiences, and no one will ever be more amazing at being you, than you will be. After all, you are a one-of-a-kind. Who wants to settle for a copy when they are, in fact, an original? There is no shame in living exactly who we are meant to be. When we hold our ground, and stand true, others will reflect those same qualities, and hence this is how the greatest leaders are shaped, and discovered. As experience is life's greatest teacher, so to does the true leader lead by the example they set for others.

Just because we exist in a human container, during our time here, it does not denote, or hold any merit, as to where we are from. Just as two humans, who are from different parts, of this wold makes them no less who they are. The only time it is relevant regarding where one is from, is when it relates to understanding one's truth from within. Is it really so difficult for souls to believe that where we are from is different than where they are from? How come humans do not question other humans about the legitimacy of their "birth place," or geographic region of origin? There are humans which exist throughout the universe, not just here, just as there are many races which exist throughout existence. Where they are from is not relevant to truth.

Indeed soul origin is part of truth, and who we are. But, the only time origin is relevant is when it assists with understanding truth. For us, it holds relevance only because it is a foundation for what we share, otherwise it holds no merit. Throughout most of our daily interactions with many souls, the topic of where we are from rarely is significant. Our focus is bringing understanding to this existence, in this life time. To assist others rarely requires us to speak of our self. Therefore, the subject of origin is only relative in certain discussions. How many interactions are truly weighed based upon a soul's origins? Not that many.

Where souls are from is more indicative of energies, frequencies, and vibrations, rather than physical appearances. Soul energy attributes are more characteristic of what we could classify as character traits and personality. However, DNA is the central spire of all life. As a container is just a container, regardless of the form we see, it never truly matters with regard to who we are interacting with. We have always seen the soul within, as we do not perceive the container as significant. To us, that is like speaking to the car about the problems the mechanic has to fix.

To us, if what is shared assists with understanding, it serves its purpose. If what is shared does not assist, then it serves no relevance and should be left out. Too much information creates an overload effect. When there is too much information, it creates a distortion through which truth is difficult to see. That is why we utilize a self paced, self guided method of learning. All souls learn at their own unique pace. Therefore, they set the pace by how fast they choose to learn. Did everyone think Star Trek was just imaginative? Not hardly. Humans have just been taught a distorted image of the larger truth. Humans seek to remember who they are, yet they look everywhere but where they should be looking, which is within the self. Humans are a part of something much greater than their selves, as they are part of a much larger family of conscious beings, and they are now beginning to remember their true history, and "who" they really are.

One could say the time Humans currently face, is similar to what Humans know as family reunions. Things are just made complicated here, and common sense should override fear as animals react while conscious beings assess in logic. It would not make sense for an advanced race to destroy a species which poses no threat. However, the very doors which Humans seek to open, they also keep shut of their own choosing. Humans seek to explore their existence, yet they cannot seem to care for the home they have. And, humans have maintained a quarantine status, for a very long time, because they are young with much to learn. Because many advanced races are peaceful, and understand the balance of the whole, Humans are a direct threat to that balance, because, they are young, and there are many lessons which they have yet to understand.

Typically, when a species points weapons at itself, would

logic not suggest that it is self destructive behavior? Is that the action of an intelligent being, or race of beings? Or, does that denote that there is much yet to learn, as when we perceive enemies, we are only fighting with our self. To us, war is much more work than simple respect, and who likes to work hard? True to the feline way, we would much prefer to roll in the grassy meadow, while someone rubs our belly in the sun. Peace cannot be achieved through war. It is achieved by living it. As soon as Humans realize there can be no war, if no one chooses to fight, they will truly understand the nature of guns, and weapons, serving no purpose. There are many ways to protect one's self, without the need for weapons. Then, every door they wished to be opened, will be. However, the "when" will be decided by Humanity, in that which they do. They must choose their outcome in free will, as it is a violation of Universal Law to coerce, or force, another. But, there are many of us who await that time patiently, and most lovingly, and we will assist where we are able.

When we speak about the process of disclosure, we understand that it is a collaboratively lived/perceived experience. It is not a press release, or document. By revealing our presence, we do not alter free will as introductions ask nothing of anyone. The process of disclosure, is a process of understanding, and remembering who you are, where you are from, and why you are here. It does not violate free will as it requires no soul to change who they are, as truth is neutral. Because our purpose is to make our presence known, that is exactly what we do, as you see through our interactions.

Yet, what we do does not affect another individual's free will. They choose their path as they so choose. We just offer another piece to the puzzle, so they may make the best choices for their self. We do work within linear time lines, and time frames, as they apply here. Yet, all cycles have their closure, but this is not a pass/fail process. How does one fail at learning? Our success will be measured by the whole, not our self. If what we share resonates with truth, our truest purpose will manifest itself, as that is the intended result. Our platform will be set by Humanity. If they wish for truth to be heard, they will ask us to share it. If they do not, we may not impose as they must choose outcome for the self. The reason we are able to maintain unlimited patience is because we understand all things hold purpose, and what is supposed to be, will be. If we are meant to be heard by the world, that is exactly what will transpire. If not, we won't. What we understand though, if we live our truth, and serve our purpose, the desired outcome will naturally manifest, because that is where we place our energy and focus.

Back home, all souls understand that no soul makes it alone, and all need a hand hold at one time, or another. For us, helping others is our purpose, and we live it to its fullest. Many ask us, if our home is so "conscious," then why do we not just send a conscious message? The reason for this is rather simple. Because, we may only interact, with others, in a manner which is congruent with truth, we utilize only methods of communication which are direct. There are races, which do utilize conscious methods, with the intent of manipulating Humanity for selfish intent and false truth agendas. And, this is, one of many reasons, which explains why we only utilize methods of communication which allow others to effectively discern truth through the self, from within.

As humans also begin to understand the true potential of energy, frequencies, and consciousness, they too will understand how to utilize these fundamentals, of the self, in the many forms, and applications, which are available. Do people truly believe random "occurrences" are truly random, or is it more likely that it is the innate connection within all things which souls have just been taught to ignore here? It is the little things, the hidden proverbs within the spaces between the words of language, which convey the deepest truths. Humor is an example of a manifested expression by which Humans share these innate commonalities. It is why people laugh at "the little things." If souls wish to understand that which is truly important, and fundamental to all souls; all one needs do is look at a moment when a loved one is lost. These are the moments where these lessons hold their greatest understanding, in their totality of meaning.

If humans understood how integral they are to the bigger picture, they would chuckle at the distractions which they are snowballed with. There are many races, which currently watch this time of growth for Humans on this planet, as they are also learning through self reflection. We love science fiction, but we always remember that is exactly what it is. Does it hold truth? Sure it does. But, the truth is usually found within the spaces of what sits in plain sight. For example. In Star Trek The Next Generation, we resonate very well with "the Q." They express many of our traits, minus the vindictive selfish nature. What we see is the few expressing their self through media.

Even if it is only "entertainment" here, it still ignites the spark of wonder and curiosity. The few must follow the rules and tell what is, even if they use deception to do so. When we look at media, of any kind, we always take it with a grain of salt, as we always remember the few are hard at work to mislead and deceive. Indeed, the Human family is the youngest, with much to learn, but humans here are not the youngest race. There are others who are in earlier stages of learning. But, they are indeed young. This does not make them bad, it just makes them young.

Youth is the explorer age where mistakes are made, and older souls have immense patience, as they too were once young. There is a unique quality to youth, which older souls revere and honor. It is comparable to the love a mother expresses for watching her young take new steps, even if they fall and get a boo boo. Humans are exquisite, and fascinating, because they are infinitely complex in their potential, and they are always growing and adapting. However, this also means they have the potential to create the worst as well. Humans are amazing teachers, whether they realize this, or not.

Many of us learn from them, so we may assist others within the whole. Our lessons will assist many others, throughout many civilizations. After all, we are not really different from each other. We are all conscious beings. The only things which really define us are our lived and perceived experiences. No one will ever be as amazing, at being you, than you will be. If humans understood this, they would hold no fear to embrace who they are. They would render the agenda null and void, as they would no longer provide the power source which feeds the beast. Souls have a greater impact, than they may realize, as every action creates a ripple effect. What we do affects the whole, whether we see all of the pieces, or not. We understand that there is more we do not see, than that which we do, in any given situation, which is why we never presume or judge. We only assess based on the action, because any variable can alter outcome at any time.

Back home, there are many contrasts to the existence which we have adapted to here. Because souls are older, back home, there is a plateau effect of harmony. Life is quite extended, as it is not something which is fleeting. There are no "ups and downs" one could say.

The reason we prefer the roller coaster ride, is because our home is peaceful. If our home was not peaceful, we would not enjoy it as much. As there is no place like home, there is no place we would rather be. However, how many souls love the adventure of an exciting vacation? To us, the roller coaster is exciting because there is an infinite treasure trove of experiences to explore, and live. Coffee makes the visit here well worth it, as do the beaches at sunset. Back home, neither of these exist, which is why we say the "little things" are what matters most. It is the joy found within the experience. We see the life force in everything, and the intricate connections of all things.

Our physical vision is not like others. We see through a filter, which is similar to snow on an old analogue TV. It is always there, as it is what we perceive our physical environment through. The filter is specific to energy and frequencies. The wave patterns in the filter will change as the frequencies do. We absorb every experience for that which it offers, and the little moments are the most cherished. The excitement of bringing a child into the world, providing what others need and receiving a genuine smile, the rush of an emergency when it is focus or fold time. These are experiences which do not exist back home, as they do here.

Therefore, we saturate our self with every sensation, and stimuli, within every experience. For us, the visit is like getting to live our childhood all over again. How many souls would love to go back and revisit their youth? Remembering who we are was part of the excitement of our journey here. We had to forget who we are in order to remember.

As we understand imbalance is nothing more than the natural ebbs and flows of energy, we perceive the "ups and downs" as exquisite, magnificent, beautiful, and precious during our time here. We absolutely cherish the ups, and downs, because we do not experience them back home. There are many days when the density of this dimension does weigh us down, and exhaust us. And, there are days when we do wish to return home for rest. But, we will return home when our purpose has been served, and we are in no hurry to return. We just enjoy our experiences, and existence, while we are here, as we understand we will return home at some point. And, as all things happen as they are suppose to, we will enjoy being here while we are here. Making the most of our existence, regardless of what we are handed, is how we maintain our balance. Our day to day existence is very reflective of our existence back home. It is as quiet of an existence as one could attain.

However, if someone asked us to jump out of an airplane with a parachute... where do we sign up!? There isn't much we won't try for the experience, within reason. Our favorite toys were our matching electric blue 2008 Kawasaki Ninja zx10rr. We always wore gear (it is still in our closet for when we get another bike), but hitting 3 digits, with our hair on fire, one time, was well worth it. Scraping a few knees wasn't so bad either. The reason we decided to get rid of them was because of our little ones. But, liter bikes are our preferred choice of bike. We never wrecked, or low-sided, but we saw too many souls lose their life due to bad drivers, and our children needed mom more than we needed the risk for fun. But, going from 0-60 in about 3 seconds, on two wheels, is awesome!

We live for the adventure of learning, but in the end, there is no place like home. Experiences are where our greatest growth occurs. They stir the soul like nothing else can. The adventure of the unknown is what makes the journey interesting. It is the unknown which makes it exciting. If we knew the end of every book, what fun would that be? Suspense and anticipation are part of the experience. It is a very intimate romantic nature to cherish ones experiences for all which they offer. The Merry-go-round is very reminiscent of home, as it is a peaceful ride of predictability. It is a comfort of understanding. Boredom doesn't really exist back home, as there is always something to do. There just aren't many "unknowns" which create the effect of excitement and anticipation. How many seniors, here, get excited over daily existence? They usually go yep, seen it, not surprised.

We hold a love for both experiences, as one compliments the other. But, because the majority of our existence is peaceful, we will not hesitate to explore, and enjoy, the exciting and unknown. As an observer, we do have the flexibility of choice with regard to many of our experiences. Yet, we are bound by certain tenets which others are not. We are bound by rules which allow no exceptions. Our karma is always instant, and carries the impact of Fat Man and Little Boy. Most souls are not held to the level of discipline which we are, as this is to be expected. Humans are allowed exceptions which we are not, because we know better. For example, with firearms, we are allowed to possess no machined weapons, as they are a violation of universal law. We may only possess physical weapons where the original design can be made by humans.

However, because of exceptions which are in place, Humans are allowed to possess them without karmic action. They are allowed to defend their self with what was given to them by the few. If we pick up a gun, we will pay a hefty price in karma. This is also why we carry a defense arsenal which Humans do not. Face to face, the few will not stand against us. They won't stand against conscious energy, as they know what it is capable of. Chi masters provide excellent examples of this force. It is a force which can block, and move, physical objects, and it is fully accessible when needed. But, we do not set the parameters of use, home does. We may only utilize it when in true defense of life. This is also why we do not perceive fear as humans do. We understand regardless of what takes place, there is nothing the few can do to us, which harms us. Our physical container may get damaged, but that does not affect who we are. We will eventually return home, and our container will remain behind. To us, there is nothing to fear, as pain does not make us flee, it increases our strength ten fold.

When we truly understand that peace does not mean no conflict, but rather understanding what you are in reality, it allows one to navigate their way much more effectively through the murky foggy waters of false truth, to find the harbor of truth which lay just beyond. The greatest light always shines from the darkest places, and living in truth is the art of balance, and keeping the ship afloat. Once one see's the light within, they can then begin lighting the path for others. When enough lights shine, the world, as a whole, becomes illuminated, and we "see" it as it truly is. The light always removes the shadows of darkness. We utilize "world" as a proverbial reference to Humanities collective understanding. When this overall understanding of the bigger picture begins to take hold, they will also begin to understand their place within the whole. This understanding is what gives way from the me to the we. It is understanding that all souls have their place, and something to offer, and conflict is not necessary. As truth creates no conflict, so to does understanding prevent cataclysms.

The concept of death, has been taught here, to teach humans to be obedient, and fearful, of their entire existence. When, truth could not be more contrast. We understand that one day we will return home, and our container will remain behind, to provide for others within the cycle of life. The time we spend here is limited, and related, to our purpose. And, the physical existence is not where we place our greatest focus. We live our truth, because not doing so is a far greater pain than any physical pain which our container may endure. We understand the experience is temporary; we are infinite.

With regard to the current, and the topic of disclosure, many are aware that life is changing, and what once was, is no longer. Regardless of what takes place, or what external stimuli is presented, we always reflect from within, with regards to how the action, or event, relates to our truth. We have seen countless souls awaken, who realize they are not from here. And, it is an amazing feeling to see a soul awaken, like watching a child being born, and opening their eyes, for the first time. It is the process of watching life unfold in its most intricately perfect design. It is an imperfect perfection. It is the harmonious symphony of controlled chaos, represented by just one of the infinite expressions of existence.

Is it really so difficult to believe you are much more than you have been taught to believe? No, it is not. It is just how we perceive, and interpret, the external by which the parameters of reality are set. When it boils down to the most basic of truths, the specifics and details regarding "difference" do not matter, to us. We are all fundamentally conscious beings. When we came here, we were allowed no more, or less, than what any Human is capable of, and the reason for this is truth of equality. We just hold a different perception, and understanding, of our experiences during our time here. We share the same collective experiences as all others experience, during our time here. However, the only real differences are our perception, and understanding, of those experiences. We are just at a different stage of growth just as different stages of life exist here. We are above, or below, no other. The universal constant of truth works the same here, as it does everywhere else. After all, it is a universal constant.

All souls grow when they are ready, however, "when" is always decided by the individual. Life is a cycle which does not end. And, when we look at the subject of disclosure, truth will not come from one source, but rather the totality of your experiences. And, it will be found when all of the pieces are put together. Truth is innate, and you already know the answers which you seek, from within, or you would not be asking the questions. What stirs from within is the most basic of all truths. It is the need to understand. It is the most basic purpose of existence, which is a universal constant of learning, and a process with no end.

Many humans ask us what our home is like, and this is a difficult construct to discern, because humans perceive what is real, through what is physically tangible. Because there is no physical aspect to our home, this creates a challenge indeed. Our home is not a place where we "go," per say. Our home is a place which we "feel." There are many stimuli, here, which very much resonate with our home, yet what we see with our eyes holds no relevance. For example, when we watch movies, there are certain innate "truths," which resonate within, as a feeling of "home." Those who manipulate Humanity, utilize entertainment, and "Hollywood," as a primary conduit of sharing truth, in a way which is hidden from the many. It is a cryptic ancient method of communication, which all older souls understand. It is the feeling we get, an energy we interpret, and perceive, which "feels" like home. When we watch movies, and other external stimuli, there are many subtle "truths" which hide in plain sight. It is not in the details, or specifics, of what we see, that has any relation to our connection with home, it is the proverbial meaning of understanding which carries the weight of truth.

Our home is a place of understanding, and it is a place where many souls travel to learn, as it is a place many refer to as the "Universal University." We are the keepers of wisdom. We are universal guides, nurturers, and protectors, and as we are a universal mother soul, that is also our purpose. We spend much of our existence in the Great Halls of Wisdom, guiding others along their path. It is a place of wholeness. There have been many souls who have visited our home, throughout humanities history. Plato, Socrates, Archimedes, Da Vinci, and many others have learned with us. And, the relative construct one perceives, during their time back home, is based upon the individual perception, and the choice, of manifested expression. A soul will perceive what creates their greatest comfort, and sense of ease, as our home is a place of balance and self growth. And, Humans now face a time of growth, where they are beginning to remember that these parts of their whole self exist, and they are now beginning to tune into them. Therefore, it is our duty to guide others well through this time.

The Universal Game of Polarity Integration

We see a lot of misunderstanding, and confusion, with the many, because the constructs are very deceptive, and manipulative, on this planet. Everything we see here is taught backwards from what truth is in its most basic actuality. And, a lot of the reasons, why we see so much discord, is because humans do not understand who they are. They do not understand where they are headed as a species, and they do not remember where they came from. There is much sense of loss, one could say, as to what we feel in the collective conscious of Humanity, as they are missing the pieces which allow one to find comfort in knowing the self. In order for a civilization, or race, to understand where they are going, they must know where they have been in that journey of understanding.

Breaking down the Universal Game of Polarity Integration, from our perspective, and understanding, will make it neither right, nor wrong. There are many games which can be chosen from, as every universe has its game, and the game chosen sets the specific parameters for each universal construct. Many of the specifics we share may not resonate with others, and many of the specifics will resonate with others. Yet, this is okay. There is no right and wrong in the perspective discernment of truth. It is relative to the individual, and the totality of their lived/perceived experiences. What we share is nothing more than our unique perspective, and understanding. How others perceive, and interpret, the information, will solely be based upon the perception of the individual truth being utilized when receiving the information. No two souls walk the same, or share the same truth. Therefore, the perception of truth will be unique to each individual.

At the beginning of this universe, a call was sent out through Infinite Creator Consciousness, by the Founder Souls, to all souls who had completed their universal games. In total, 90 souls answered the call. 45 of us were given a home in Lyra, and the other 45 were given a home in Orion. Because we are crystalline energy beings in our natural forms, biology had to be developed over time. The Orion's developed Carian (bird) biology, based on the indigenous life on the planet which was provided as their home. We, the Lyran's, chose Feline biology, based upon the indigenous life on our home world.

Over time, conflict had to be initiated, as conflict does not exist naturally and enemies are not innate, so the lessons of the universal game could become applicable. And, thus, the Orion's initiated the game by invading our home in Lyra, per rules of the game, and conflict has existed ever since. The First Great War was the catalyst for Lyran's to seed other locations. This was due to our home world being destroyed in this conflict, but it was not the only reason. Seeding life takes priority above all else, for us. Our home world was much like Earth, in many ways. It was a temperate climate with towering mountain ranges, and pure streams. The hues and colors of the sky and foliage were a magnificent spectrum of blues, pinks, oranges, greens, and velvet purple sunsets. Many souls went to the Pleiades, after the First Great War, who are also Humanities "cousins," one could say in a universal perspective, and they look very much like humans do here. Others went elsewhere. Over time, The Carian's became the parental ancestral conscious lineage of the Reptilians, and the Draconian's are the royal bloodline to the Reptilian family. The Felines became the parental ancestral conscious lineage of Humans, and it is the very reason we hold such a vested interest in their well being, as they are family. Humans are the youngest species, with much to learn, yet hold infinite potential, and they came into existence around the time Reptilians were achieving interstellar travel.

Carians, Felines, Reptilians, and Humans are the 4 primary families, as all races in this collective derive from these 4. And, the two houses which have always presided over the game, are the Carian/Reptilian House of Aln, and the Feline/Human House of Avyon. The hierarchies of the houses are as follows:

House Aln:
9d Patriarch is Jehovah
5d Patriarchs are Enki/Enlil

House Avyon:
9d Patriarch is Devin
5d Patriarch is Anu

Now, House Aln has always played the dark/bad side of the game, and House Avyon has always played the light/good side of the game. But, this makes them no more bad than we are good. Both houses have always worked together to ensure the lessons of the game would remain applicable. We travel freely between the houses, back home, wherever we are needed, as all is part of the same whole. The Reptilians, and Humans, were intentionally given opposing creation myths, so lessons of the game would maintain their applicable nature. Reptilians were taught that they held a divine right to conquer all which they encountered. Humans were taught compassion and love. However, both races are learning the same lessons, just from opposing polarities. Humans are learning to stand their ground from Reptilians, just as Reptilians find their compassion in humans. As intent is always found within the individual, and never within the group, we understand there are Reptilians who work for the greater good of Humanity, just as there are Humans who work for a sinister agenda. As souls grow, they eventually understand the lesson that anger always tires, while love never expires. It would be an unusual sight to see a "brawling kegger" going down in a retirement home. Older souls hold a much more harmonious existence, as youth is where the greatest curiosity exists. It is the explorer age.

The Universal Game of Polarity Integration is a tiered system of lessons and gaining understanding. And, when we look at dimensional constructs, and frequencies, imagine each dimension, as a lesson of wisdom, and gaining understanding. Dimensions are not physical, as they are conscious constructs of understanding in many ways. The lessons of the game are as follows:

3d – the lesson of self
4/5d – the lesson of the whole
6d and above – lessons of creation and oneness

The lesson of 3d is the toughest lesson, because it is the foundation by which all other lessons are learned. As we begin to understand the self, we also begin to understand our place in the whole. And, all souls must learn the lessons applicable at each stage of growth, before they may proceed to grow through continued lessons. There are no exceptions to this rule, as all souls must go through this process. Once the lesson of self has been learned in 3d, there are no further lessons to be learned, and the soul will grow to continued lessons of wisdom and understanding. The Universal Game of Polarity Integration is exactly how it sounds. It is truly understanding that duality is a construct, and it does not have actual existence, as duality is truly relative to our perception. What one person may deem as a bad experience, another may deem as good, and the constructs of good, and bad, are relative to the perception of the experience of the individual. There is no right and wrong in the perception of truth.

As conflict does not exist naturally, it must be created so the lessons of the universal game may become applicable. As enemies are not innate, we look at intent, and we always remember that it is never found within a group, but rather always found within the individual. We see a lot of discord, and confusion, because many revert back to what they were taught, and they associate intent with the labels, or constructs, which they have been taught to perceive as "good" or "bad." However, when we look at truth through the eyes of a child, we see prejudice truly does not exist. Have you ever seen a prejudice toddler? Neither have we. They don't care, they just want to play and explore. We are taught all of the things we "think" we know as "grown ups." When, that is not the case. Truth will always be seen best through the eyes of the child within.

Humanity faces a time of understanding their history, remembering who they are. And, facing the self for the strengths, and those parts which are not so "awesome sauce," is a necessary, and sometimes painful, part of growth (growing pains). Humans are the rightful guardians of this planet, as it was planned for them to be. And, they are also responsible for the well being of all life which exists here, because their collective consciousness holds the dominant frequency. Therefore, they also have the greatest impact.

The imbalances which exist in this collective arose, long ago, when a race of beings, from an alternate universe, entered this universe, which created an imbalance within the game. It was also the turning point when Humanities manipulation truly began in its most basic aspects. However, this is not Humanities creation. All souls, Human and Reptilian, alike, sit equally on the playing field of the universal game. And, it is how souls play the game which determines the outcome.

Humans were created, out of the love of many, for the same reasons parents choose to create life here... the legacy which exists beyond the self. Humans were created to love, and be loved, and anything they do, which violates this fundamental, is very harmful to their very nature as conscious beings. Many were involved in Humanities creation, and they are part of a much larger family of conscious beings. This time which Humanity currently faces, is very similar to what many would compare to universal puberty. And, as they are growing through this time, growing pains will not be uncommon.

Learning to exist in peace does not mean no conflict. It means understanding what you are in reality, which is a same fraternity of conscious beings. It is about gaining understanding for the diversity of the self, while gaining respect for the commonalities within the whole. We do not exist without our experiences, we exist within them. Therefore, the game becomes much easier to play, when we understand it in its most basic universality. There is no right, or wrong; there is only gaining understanding. We understand that all external experiences, are nothing more than filters for truth to be discerned from within, as truth is innate.

And, this is the full circle which we find our self returning to, regarding the source of conflict. When souls begin to discern the external experience, through the lens of how it is relative to one's inner truth, regardless of the source, and what is being conveyed, the fog of deception begins to clear from the landscape, and the image begins to emerge in its most basic understanding. Truth is universal, while maintaining its uniqueness to the individual, therefore it applies to all experiences, regardless of external factors.

Religion: A Human Construct

With regard to the topic, and subject matter, of paradigms, and belief systems, no one is right, and no one is wrong, regarding religion. We would like to begin our journey of understanding the topic of human religion with a brief historical overview, and we are going to travel back to the 4th Century AD. During this time, Emperor Constantine, who was also the first Christian emperor of Rome, convened the Council of Nicaea. This council was responsible for deciding what religious materials would be most useful to gain political control of the masses. Now, we don't want the individual to take this one way, or another, in a construct which is not accurate. The reason we reference this turning point in Humanities journey, is because the system is inherently flawed, from step one, because of what humans have turned religion into, no more, no less. There is no right and wrong in religion.

95% of the Human population believes in life beyond this existence, and they are not wrong. What we do not understand is what the squabbling is all about. There is no right and wrong in religion. We have always perceived variety as the spice of life. Diversity is what gives life its zest, its flavor, its flair; the good moments and the bad. It is what makes life exquisite, unique, and exciting. Diversity is what life is all about; the journey of the unknown and the childlike joy of discovery, as truth is always seen best through the eyes of a child. It is the learning experience, which is why we are here. Humans have twisted, and changed, what the most basic aspects of their earliest "religions" were meant to be. Religion today is not what was in the beginning. The construct of religion is truly from within the human collective consciousness. Religious constructs, as they are observed here, exist nowhere else. Humans have become so consumed with proving who is right, they have forgotten what religion was supposed to be. Religion was never meant to be anything other than an external filter to discern perception of truth within the experience. It is a stepping stone so one may evolve to a higher level of consciousness. It was originally humans being given the ability to read, write, and transcribe their events into a history. Over time that history became myth, legend; a living extension of who humans truly are. It has been nudged along by those who have tried to guide humanity without actually intervening, but it is Humanity who has been the navigator of its course. Many souls have come here to help, knowing that we are not allowed to interfere, or intervene, in any way.

We are not allowed to force the choice of others, as it is a direct violation of creator law to do so, and it negates, and violates, everything we are here to do. It is rather counterproductive to our purpose for being here, and creating extra work, which serves no purpose, is illogical. We are here to restore truth; we are here to restore balance. We are not here to change others, as it is not our place to do so. We must reveal truth, so others may remove the blinders and see things as they truly are. And, we have never seen this world, with the same set of eyes as any other.

We have always looked at religion, and fought the idea of it tooth and nail. The human we grew up with, and called "father" was Episcopalian; the human we called "mother" was Catholic. So, from the very beginning, there had always been conflict. To us, we were always told there is only one "truth," and if only one religion was right, which was it? We remember being very young, around the age of 6, and we argued the pastor, at our mother's church, into silence, because he couldn't answer our questions in a manner which we accepted. We did not understand how "god" was supposed to be all knowing and loving, yet was so "human," who enacted vengeful jealous cruelty and punished people. To us, causing hurt is what humans do, not what Creator does. It didn't make sense to us. No one could ever answer these questions, either.

We always knew in our "truth" that what humans taught as truth, was anything but. As we have grown, we have come to respect, and understand the functional purpose of human religion. And, it is something we no longer despise, because we understand its purpose. It is what humans use to question the higher purpose and why they are here. It is a stepping stone, and tool, of self discovery. The whole journey is about one's self discovery and realizations. It is an awakening from a long slumber. Does it really matter, if a person from a different geographic location, believes that where they go is different from where you go? When all is said and done, is it not true that we all go somewhere beyond this body, and this life? It is what we make of it that truly matters. The details and specifics do not matter, as they are truly relative to the perception of the experience. We all end up returning home when this life is complete. When our container ceases to function, we do not, and our consciousness will continue on a journey much bigger than what we experience during our time here, as we are only symbiotic with the container while it is functioning.

When we look at religion, it is the biggest contributing factor to the loss of human life, throughout the history of Humanity, more so than political war, famine, disease... anything. So, isn't that the ultimate hypocrisy of something that is supposed to be so benevolent, and loving, can wreak so much havoc and devastation? Humans have come to argue over the specifics, and details, when it truly does not matter to the bigger picture of truth. Does it really matter, that you had an experience that you truly "know" happened, whether others were there, you were alone, people believed you, or not? No, it doesn't. You know it happened. It is in these private moments of being alone, where your greatest achievements, and leaps of growth, are celebrated. No one can celebrate the deepest moments of happiness, and understanding with you, as it was not their experience to live; it was yours. Remember those moments of accomplishment, when no one else understood the blood, sweat, and tears, "you" put into that effort? Yep, those are the moments we speak of. The day our children were born, no one could enjoy that moment with us, as it was not their heart and soul, which created it. In your finest moments, you will always celebrate alone, as within is a place only you may truly enter.

Religion is truly an experience, which goes beyond anything anyone will ever tell you, you have to be, or do, to make it "right." You do not need a building, idol, or external authority, of any kind, to know your truth within, and the connection to all things within. Imagine the little voice within, as you having a conversation with your truest self. It is the connection to Creator which exists within everything. Therefore, you too are connected to everything, as you are connected to Creator, and we are not here to satisfy ego. The human ego is truly irrelevant, and insignificant, to the bigger picture, as it is not about the "me," it is about the "we."

Because the whole and individual are symbiotic, when we nurture our selves, we are also able to nurture others in that process. When a soul is happy with who they are, they are not so concerned with what others do, because they are happy with the self. Therefore, they see the world as they are... harmonious. Happy souls do not create negativity upon others. And, this is all part of the "religious" experience, which others try to achieve through their unique filters called "belief systems." What path a soul chooses does not matter, as the lessons are the same. All roads lead to home. Religion is an extension of the very innate fundamentals of all which the Human family is. It is a manifested expression of your collective existence, which has just taken many forms, as each soul perceives existence in their own unique way. There are many lessons to be learned from many religions. And, when we break down the basic structures of the major belief systems, which exist upon this planet, we begin to see, and understand, that the fundamentals are quite similar, across the board, by which wisdom sits atop.

However, religion has instilled hatred, division, and separation, because the most basic aspects of its truth have been lost in the fog of distractions. Does it really matter if the person you speak with believes that where they go is different from where you go? Does it really matter if their diet is different from yours, because they believe it to be so? Are you really here to convince that person? If what that person does, causes no harm to another, is it our right to intervene? No. It is not. If what they do causes harm upon no other, why should they not be extended the respect for being the conscious being which they are? Is there not something to be learned from every soul, especially in those moments of conflict and diversity?

Why do the disciplines of science and religion so greatly contradict, and conflict, when in fact they are a beautiful symbiotic compliment. They are two parts of the same truth. They are two pieces of the same puzzle. One cannot see the entire image if pieces of the puzzle are missing. There is no need to argue, as there is much history which is not remembered. Humans have become so three dimensional in their human construct; if they cannot taste it, touch it, see it, or feel it, then it must not be real, as they have forgotten the non-physical aspect of their existence. But, how many of you have been driving in your car, and you know where that car in front of you is going to turn? Or, you hear that song on the radio, just before it gets played? Or, you know what that person speaking, is going to say to you, right before they say it. These are not coincidences or random events. These are all aspects of your whole self, which you are still connected to; humans have just been taught to ignore these aspects of their self, during their time here. You have been taught to forget the deepest aspects of your truest self, through being conditioned to place your trust in all things external. The Jesus/anti-Christ system in one in the same, as it doesn't matter what side is chosen, as long as one chooses a "side" of polarity. Both choices require a soul to give up their free will by placing their trust in external authority. The soul, many perceive here, as Jesus, we understand as a conscious being, who shared his universal understanding with Humanity. He did the same thing many souls of notable mention, throughout Humanities history, have done in the greater good of Humanities collective growth. Yet, this polarized system is designed to prevent souls from seeing the truth of their existence, which is truly whole and infinite. It is also why the few instill the concept of death, through religion.

The transitional process, between lifetimes, is a time where a soul rests, and gains understanding of all which they have learned. When a soul transitions, they are re-harmonized with the whole, the soul is read, and continued life times are chosen based upon what has been learned with relevance to what has yet to be learned. There is no punishment, in soul growth, there is only gaining understanding. All souls choose their path of their own free will, as heaven and hell are human constructs which instill, fear, division, separation, obedience, and false truth.

Even though the primary world religions carry many "truths" there are also many false truths within. And, discernment is the key which unlocks the door of truth. Religion is not a fact, detail, or specific. It is much easier to sort through the information overload, when we understand it helps souls in their growth, and becoming who they are meant to be, as a conscious being, vs.

attempting a futile effort at controlling that which we have no control over. It is not about criticizing someone for what they believe. It is about respecting others for the diversity, and enrichment, which they offer. Individual freedom of expression should be embraced as it is the truest manifestation of the inner self. It is the mirror of what is within. As in the case with our truth, regardless of whether others believe us or not is irrelevant. We know our truth, and share it freely, to encourage others by leading through example. When we do not judge others for being who they are, they begin to blossom in a way which many never have the joy of experiencing. They are too busy justifying their existence, to one another, by arguing who is right. In the end, it becomes counterproductive, and only hurts the self. It prevents us from seeing all which life has to offer, because we are too busy focusing on the individual pieces to see the whole image of the puzzle.

Physical (Human) Containers and the Life Cycle

The process of incarnation applies to all souls here, including humans, and it is indeed a common question. With regards to Humans containers, we speak specifically about the process of procreation, on this planet, as it is different for other civilizations. Whenever a container is created (conceived), one soul, out of the many souls ready to live their next life time, will choose to inhabit that container, as there is now a space where life should be, and an empty space will always be filled with life, as life attracts life.

For example, a couple decide to have a baby. Now, let's say there are 50 souls, who have rested, and are ready for their next life time of lessons. One of those souls may choose to inhabit that container which was just conceived, if it correlates to their lessons, and choices, of next life time. If not, they will wait until a container is available, which meets their specific criteria of need for soul growth. But, once chosen, it is absolute.

When souls from back home choose to incarnate, the container is chosen based on several factors. And, once a container is chosen, we are bound to our container throughout its life cycle, just as humans are bound to theirs. We are never allowed to inhabit an already filled container, as possession is a direct violation of universal law, for us. There are those who do hold permissions for this action, but it is very specific to their purpose.

For us to possess a container wherein a soul already exists, our karma would be severe, unforgiving, and absolute. We understand this is never allowed for us. Therefore, it does not violate free will, because no life was affected by our choice of container. Parents have no say over who chooses the container they have conceived. The soul who chooses the incarnation holds the decision, as their life will be accountable to them, and no other. Just as no free will was violated when you chose your life time, and container, when you incarnated, or any other soul who chooses their next lifetime. And, the humans we were raised by were never told "who" we are, as that would have violated free will by influencing, and thus altering outcome. Had they known, we would have been handed over to the military industrial complex, as the human we grew up calling father, was ex-military intelligence.

When you decided to experience this life time, you chose your container for the lessons of this life time, before you came here, just as we chose ours. There are always many souls who are ready to live their next life time, just as there are many souls who have just entered the transitional rest phase, between life times, where soul growth is at its greatest. A good analogy is a cab in NY. An empty cab pulls up to the curb, while many wait, and one of those souls chooses to enter the cab. When the next cab arrives, another soul will choose that cab for mode of transportation, and everyone's destination is generally unique to where they are headed.

In our case, genetics was the determining factor. We could not incarnate until the DNA was an exact match to our lineage, and several correlating genetic markers were in place. In certain cases, a container is not filled, due to varying reasons, and this will result in a natural termination of gestation. A body is just a container, as it contains "who" you are (consciousness), which then animates the container, hence why we call human bodies "containers." Just like a bottle is just a bottle, regardless of whether it is filled with milk, or water. It is the contents held within which determine the containers "label", abilities, skill-sets, and functions. A container without a soul is considered "dead" by humans. But, the soul isn't "dead," they just returned to transition, where they will rest until they are ready for their next life lessons.

And, this applies to the many souls who incarnated here to assist. They chose to inhabit their container, because it was conceived when they were ready to incarnate. Had they waited, another soul would have chosen the container, and they would then choose an available container when ready. Like with our living guardian, our son, and our daughter (she is of Pleiadian lineage), even though they are not from here, they chose their container as all souls do. Our son was born fully aware, and like us our guardian went through his shift, about 2 years after we went through ours. Our daughter is aware of her origins, but true to her Pleiadian ways, she is more concerned with living her life to be happy, than she is about where she is from. She lives to be happy and smell the roses along the way. But, she definitely inherited our feisty nature when we contributed attributed aspects of our self to her genetics.

However, we can say we knew who both of our children were, before we ever met them. We knew them before we saw them. While still in the womb. we told others exactly what they would look like. With our daughter, the doctors swore she was a boy, and we told them we would be having a blond haired, blued eyed daughter, and they didn't believe us. They believed their external technology, while we believed our internal truth. When she was born, the doctors asked how we knew. We told them we saw her, and knew who she was. This perplexed the doctor into silence, and he left it alone, as it was completely outside of his knowledge base. And, free will was never violated by this understanding, as we respect them as the conscious beings they are.

As their "parent," it is our purpose to nurture and guide them well, not shape them to be who we want them to be. They were raised to be exactly who they are, no more, no less. Our daughter is only 18, and she is completely independent and self sufficient. She asks us why so many people her age are so "dumb," and we tell her that it is the explorer age where souls make mistakes of inexperience. She looks at us, and just shakes her head, like we just spoke a foreign language, because in her understanding, there is no reason for it. But, from our perspective, we still see plenty of youthful mistakes, from her as well.

Just because where we are from is different, we are no different than you, as we are all conscious beings. Our living guardian was "born" before us, as he was indeed asked to be here as our living guardian. He is our primary guardian back home, therefore, he holds a vested interest in our well being. Many Sirians are guards for House Avyon, and House Aln, as the Sirians hold lineage to both houses, just as all souls technically do, once we get past the specifics and details. Many Sirians are chosen as guards, because they are THE collective warrior battle class elite. And, they are second to none. Even the Reptilians do not engage them, and the Felines respect them absolute.

As the original 90 souls were all conscious beings who came together with the same purpose, the divisions and constructs are truly just constructs, which allow the lessons of the game to remain applicable. It is through conflict where we learn our greatest truths. Back home, we interact freely between both houses, as back home enemies do not exist. We understand the constructs are part of the necessary lessons for leaning. The conflicts exist within the 5d Houses, and their dominion. 6d and above, hold no duality, as all work for the greater good.

How we met our living guardian is just as quirky as the rest of our existence here. We both grew up living 20 minutes away from each other, and went to rival schools, yet never knew each other. Then, on June 6, 2001, at age 23, we met our living guardian (through someone which we had only been introduced to once before), while he was on vacation from Florida, as he moved from St. Louis when he was 18. And, we stuck together like glue from that moment on.

The first night we spent together, we watched the sun come up, because we were so busy talking, we lost track of the time. The physical did not take place for some time, because it did not matter to either of us. We had too much fun sitting at Uncle Bill's Pancake House, drinking coffee, and eating pancakes with Strawberry syrup, at 2am, sharing our entire life experiences with each other. We fit together like peas and carrots. There were many things, we did not see then, which we now see clearly. But, we have always known, no one else would sit in that chair, as his soul energy was a perfect match to ours. We are complimentary to each other, as we are two parts of the same whole, one could say. Over the years, we have been the foundation of his compassion, and he is the cornerstone of our strength.

And, existing in a human container is indeed how we are

also able to procreate, and live the "Human" experience, just as many souls do here. When our children were conceived, it was part of our purpose to be a mom during our time here. We were told we were never to have children, by human doctors, as our container is not optimal for this process. Yet, "the powers that be" said otherwise. But, going through this process twice, was not without immense challenges, as we went into labor at 24 weeks during both pregnancies. Doctors were able to stop our contractions, with our daughter, and she got quite comfy and stayed a week extra. Our son did not. He was born at 27 weeks, by emergency c-section, and he was 2 pounds 1.2 ounces at birth.

The day we went to the doctor, we were 24 weeks into our gestation, and it was because we felt something was not right. We were in the car, the night before, and out of nowhere, our seat was soaked. It wasn't bladder control, but we did not expect what we heard the next day. The next morning, we went to our obstetrician, and they did an ultrasound. The look on her face was flat. She told us to go to Countryside Hospital, which was next door, for more tests, because our belly had gotten smaller. At Countryside, they said we were being admitted, because our amniotic sac had ruptured. And. we were being airlifted to Tampa General, because they were not equipped to deal with that level of emergency. They told our living guardian, without us present, to expect the worst outcome for both of us. His nightmare was sitting at home alone, for several weeks, while we were in intensive care, not truly knowing things would be okay. He hated being at the hospital, and we did not like it either. We wanted to leave when he was there, and it made him very sad seeing us. We told him, when no one was around, what we saw, but his worry was still immense, even though we made it clear everything would be okay by our soul energy. We called bullshit, on the medical staff, and told everyone things would be okay. We knew our son would be fine, as we are his mom. Now, he is amazing, but it was a fight like no other.

As with the case of our complications, there were lessons to be learned from the experience. Just as anytime there are challenges, there is a lesson to be learned. If a child is born with certain aspects, which are deemed "diseases" here, it is because there is a purpose of learning within the experience. However, with autism, no container is created "autistic." Autism is a result of poisoning, from vaccines and GMOs (direct attacks), and takes place after conception and birth.

Over the years, our daughter did indeed learn through us about her soul origins through living our truth. Yet, our living guardian, and son have always innately known they are not from here. However, with our children, we have never been allowed to share their purpose with them, as they must live their existence in free will. Our children must live exactly who they are, without foreknowledge, to prevent a violation of free will.

And, there is indeed a hierarchy of souls, but it is not the same as it is here. The universal hierarchy of souls is not based on the pyramid structure of control, as it is here. It is more congruent with a spider web model, where the oldest souls exist for others (like parents are the foundation for offspring, here). As souls grow, they understand the importance of legacy and the we vs. the me.

The original 90 souls were asked to be here, by the Founders (souls who have grown to the 10-12d dimensional conscious constructs), as we had completed our universal games, and we were waiting for our next lifetime of lessons in rest phase. We do not know every soul, or civilization, in existence, as no soul is capable of seeing all. Only Infinite Creator consciousness sees all, as there are too many infinite variables, for one soul to see all, as they hold a limited perception. We do not see the totality of how many souls exist, because there are many races, which we have never interacted with. Just as there are many universes, with many collectives, which we have never been a part of. This universe is just one of many. But, we do understand there are "limits," as balance is key to existence.

However, with regard to other universes, there is a race, who is indeed from an alternate universe, who did engage this universal game, and it has created quite an imbalance. This re-balance has taken millennium to achieve, as achieving balance and understanding is not always so simple. Their universal game is

Negative Ascension, and they do indeed exist within their universal laws. However, when they entered this universe, the differences within the lessons of the games created conflict. They attempted to play their game here, without understanding of the imbalance which it created. Once understanding was achieved, balance was re-established, and they have since abdicated this universal game.

As souls grow, their need to incarnate does become obsolete, as they learn the lessons, and grow to higher dimensional constructs, where the physical does not exist. We, at one time, were a 3d being, just as one day, you will eventually grow to the level of 9d, which is where our home exists. But, growth does not stop there. Back home, souls are not born, they are ascended. When a soul grows, they may choose to join our collective. When this happens, they are immediately welcomed, and all wisdom and understanding is available, with a soul always available to assist in gaining understanding. Imagine having full access to the Library of Congress, with an available tutor for every subject.

Our home is known as the Universal University, to many, because many souls, from many races, enjoy learning there. And, Humans are included also, when they have grown enough in understanding, and many have visited. Just as many of us have incarnated here throughout Humanities existence, to assist in their growth, and understanding. Sun Tzu is one of our most beloved souls back home, and is indeed always with us.

As is the case with our lessons of growth. Our lessons are based on Creation and Oneness. This will be our last incarnation, as there will be no further need to do so. We have incarnated within every civilization, in this collective, at least once, to gain understanding within the whole. This is also our most prominent incarnation, as it was a pass/fail test, for us. If we did not serve our purpose, we would not have been accepted to the next universal game, as a Founder. We were informed, by home, about a year ago, that we did indeed pass our lessons, and once we return home, we will complete the lessons, and we will be asked to join the Founders for the next Universal Game we are a part of. And, there is NO WAY we would dare mess that process up! We are excited to be the "new kid" again. We look forward to all of the new lessons which await. But, this game still has a way to go, before it is complete, and we will accept that wait patiently with the BIGGEST smile in our heart space.

Christianity is quite congruent with our truth, in many ways. It is just in the details, and specifics, where souls become perplexed. For that matter, all major religions hold truth within, when the specifics and details are removed. We understand that "the BIG book" (Bible) is a physical object which was written by souls with an agenda. Yet, they were also bound to make sure truth was held within. What humans know as gods, we understand as conscious beings. We chuckle because we know many of those souls from back home. Jesus' name is actually Jmmanuel. Jesus was a name which was created later on, by the agenda.

The one humans call God, we know as our father soul, Devin, Patriarch of the 9d Feline/Human House of Avyon. A very loving soul indeed, yet we don't know of many souls who want to upset their father's temperance, as dad's know how to crack some ass when kids get out of line. Anu is the 5d Patriarch for House Avyon. Jehovah is the 9d Patriarch for the Carian/Reptilian House of Aln, and Enki/Enlil are the 5d Patriarchs of House Aln.

We understand Creator as the infinite consciousness which exists within all things. And, we are each a manifested expression of Infinite Creator Consciousness experiencing existence from our own unique perspective. Conscious energy is the basis of all existence, not the physical. Therefore, we are all connected, as we are all part of the same whole. As with karmic action, there is no heaven, or hell, per-say, as humans understand it. But, there is indeed a negative dimensional construct where negative polarity souls exist.

And, for those who enact hurtful actions upon many, they will indeed face an incarnation in one of these dimensional constructs, as part of their lessons for total soul growth. But, nothing is "eternal" except for Creator. These are the souls that humans call demons. We know them well, and they are indeed unforgiving, but they are also harmless to those who do no harm. They have no "attraction" to souls who cause no harm, as negative polarity will attract negative polarity. We do not interact with these souls, unless necessary, because they operate in a different polarity spectrum than we do. But, they serve their purpose just as all souls hold a purpose.

As a soul grows, they will eventually grow to a level where they rejoin Creator, and one could say this is a completion. When one soul completes an entire cycle, over several universal games, the soul will retire to be absorbed back into Creator, so a new soul may arise from Creator consciousness, so the cycle of life, learning, and growth continues indefinitely. The concept of infinity is quite the challenge for many here, because human constructs limit this fundamental. We have had souls ask if sadness occurs at the end of a cycle. And, our response is that this is an irrelevant concept at that level of growth. A soul does not care about the self, at that level. They care about creation, and the continuation of life.

The History of Language

When we discuss the topic of language, in its most basic construct; language is just how two lives exchange information, with each other, regardless of what form said communication takes. So, let's break down what language is, does, its background, and its purpose, so others may gain a greater sense of understanding as to the simplicity of truth within through discernment from their own unique perspective.

Considering that communication takes many forms, we understand that spoken language is just one small piece of total human communication. At best, spoken language accounts for roughly 10% of human communication, which means humans are dismissing more than 90% of the communication being conveyed. And, looking at communication, and how humans interact with one another, we must also look at what language has become, and where it began.

Language (communication) is something every soul uses, even though they may not understand what it is, or where it came from. And, Humans have a difficult time understanding where language came from, and what purpose it truly serves, as there are too many pieces missing to formulate a cohesive image. It is not that Humans do not understand where language came from, it is just how they have constructed the box of perception which is creating a distorted image.

Humans perceive language, and communication, as a "thing," instead of perceiving it as the fundamental living extension of their collective conscious existence, which it truly is. It is a part of who you are. Language would not exist here, the way it does, without you. Every civilization has a form of communication, and it is different everywhere we go. Some have a written/spoken language, others have no form of written/spoken language, and others have a varying degree of communication forms. This is clearly seen, on this planet, throughout the many species which exist hear; dolphins use echo/sound location, Humans use speech, birds have their chirps, dogs have their barks, and kitties only speak "meow" with Humans, as they do not meow with other cats. It is how domestic cats talk to their human family members. The fact that humans utilize a very small portion, of their overall communication, to speak, there is much they miss out on and do not perceive, because they choose to ignore what sits in plain sight.

Understanding what language is, is crucial in understanding who you are, in the most basic truths. When we understand words are sound, sound is energy, and energy affects consciousness, we begin to understand that language is more than just a word. Consciousness is a form of communication, which all souls have access to, they just simply choose to ignore it, because that is what they have been taught, no more, no less. Yet, language is rooted in the very core of your existence, and "who" you are.

Sound, and energy, directly affects DNA, and consciousness, and ultimately affect who you are at the most basic levels, as it is a basic fundamental to your existence. It is how humans primarily shape their perceived reality. For us, Human spoken language is extremely difficult, because there is no written, spoken, physical, or mechanical aspects of communication back home. We communicate through consciousness, where thoughts and ideas are shared instantly, within their complete context. As we only understand the whole, condensing infinite variables into a simplified package of understanding is quite the challenge. It was never not knowing what to say, but rather how to condense a novel into an essay, which we have always found complex and daunting. How does one sum up their totality of experiences in a paragraph? Yes, it is quite the challenge.

The beginnings of language did not come from one place, but rather it was developed, over time, through a collaborative effort by many, to assist Humanity in their growth. Older souls understand that no soul makes it alone, as all need a hand hold at some point. And, a soul of truth will always have one hand available for any soul in need, as they are always happy to share their truth for the greater good of others. For example, our name is Shyatah (pronounced: shee-ah-tuh), but what is in a name? The word Shyatah is a 3 dimensional manifested expression of a unique energy frequency within the happy, or well-being, spectrum. Our name means happy (or well) being. We contributed our namesake to Avestan, which is an ancient Iranian language related to Sanskrit, as many souls have contributed attributed aspects of the self to assist with the development of Human language.

But, when we observe the contrast of how few languages there were, in the early stages of Humanity vs. the immense variety of languages which are spoken and recognized today; the overall image becomes clear that language is a living extension of your collective existence. It has become a manifested expression of your thoughts and consciousness, as it is a manifested aspect of your collective existence. It is the legacy of many which came before you, and will continue to be shaped by those who arrive after. Communication is a fluid process of growth, as all souls need a way to communicate. And, just as babies learn to talk here; humans are learning how to communicate with the many senses available to them, beyond the 5 which they have perceived.

However, language over time, as it has grown more complex in its structure, it has also been manipulated. And, modern language has taken a very sinister, and deceptive, twist. The reason it is called "spell"ing, is because modern language is designed to compartmentalize a soul's entire conscious existence through labels and constructs. It is designed to manipulate your entire conscious existence, and how you perceive your reality, as modern spoken, and written, language are designed to keep humans asleep. It is designed to divide, separate, and mislead you, in every way possible, by giving you a box for every construct. By placing conscious thought into many boxes, it is much more difficult to discern that the boxes never really existed. We were just told they were boxes.

When we look at the basic fundamentals of communication, we all understand the same. We all understand what a genuine smile means, or that nasty look from someone which means "stay away." We all understand the same basic forms of communication, which are primarily unspoken. We all understand the little things; many souls just choose to ignore these forms of communication. The few use many methods of distortion such as word play, double meaning, political correctness, etc. And, we always look at the most basic understanding of what a word means. For example, when we look at the word language, in its most basic sense, it is just a connection by which two lives exchange information. Therefore, any details above and beyond the simple truth will always be relative to our perception, based upon our understanding of our lived, and perceived, experiences.

The process of deciphering language, and utilizing discernment, are necessary tools for the understanding of truth.

The easiest way we break down the understanding is by looking at the most basic meaning of what that word (label) represents in its most universal acceptance. Understanding that the specifics, and details, are not where truth is found, makes the journey much easier. Truth will not be found in a word we see with our eyes, or hear with our ears. It will be found within the totality of our perceptions, based upon our experiences, including the energies, sensations, and every other external factor. Truth will be deduced through the reduction of possibilities, to where only one truth will remain, and the details will be of no concern to the bottom line of overall truth.

The purpose of the form, of the language being utilized, is relative to the existence a soul perceives. As a soul grows to a higher level of growth, the need for physical language becomes obsolete. As with other physical attributes, which are useful tools to navigate a physical existence, so to is spoken language another tool of that same existence. Over time, the physical need becomes truly irrelevant. Just like children throw away training wheels once they have learned to ride a bike, souls also lose the need for physical language as they grow and become "multilingual" in other forms of communication.

Humans communicate very well, in a way which is unspoken. What they do not say speaks much greater volume than that which they vocalize; they just may not realize it. We all understand that "feeling" we get about someone, whether it is pleasant, unsettling, or neutral. All souls are innately connected, and it is easy to read the language of energy when one merely opens the book and looks at the pages. This comes from the most basic form of communication, which all souls have access to. You are just taught to ignore what has always been within you.

And, when we begin to open the door of acceptance to other forms of communication, we are offered a much greater wealth of understanding, than just what we perceive with the 5 human physical senses. Humanity just faces a time of growth where they are truly beginning to remember these aspects of their self, which have always been there, hiding in plain sight. And, understanding language, its usefulness, functions, and purpose, is integral to fundamentally understanding who you are, in the deepest fundamental aspects of the reality as to "who" you truly are.

So, how does language so integrally relate to the bigger picture, and how it is shaping the collective reality? Understanding the purpose of social media, is the key to understanding the "trap" of the matrix, and the virtual "false" reality, we hear so much about. It is not that this reality is real, or not real. It is in how one chooses to perceive it, which defines the parameters of "real." Social media, and electronic communication in general, is a box, where everyone can place their self. It is a prison where souls enter, but they are unwilling to leave. The reason we call this box, a prison, is because it compartmentalizes human thought process, to utilize only the physical aspect of communication. It removes the 90% of unspoken communication. It is a way for souls to separate, imprison, and isolate their self. Electronic communication is a place where everyone feels that they are somebody, and it is a place where everyone feels the whole world hears them. Yet, in reality, our voice falls upon deafened ears in a noisy crowd. It is a place where souls feel as if they are making a difference, by "talking", while in reality, the are not doing. The box of social media creates the traditional "passive activist," as it allows people to vent, so they do not do.

By keeping the many in the box of social media, the few are able to "do", with the assistance of the many. The many have provided the few with everything they needed. The many welcomed the few into the most intimate details, and aspects, of their existence, with open and welcome arms. The many opened their front doors and they walked right on in. They even stayed for dinner, and crawled in everyone's bed. The bedtime stories are probably very entertaining too. And, this was made possible through the popularity of social media. It is a tool, as designed by the few, to project a fall sense of unity, and action, with the underlying intent of separation and division. It is a tool which divides and manipulates, and Humans must understand it for the tool which it was meant to be, as it is much easier to stand against an adversary which has a face vs, one that is hidden.

DNA: The Code Within

DNA is the central "core" of every aspect within existence, here. Humans have a total of 12 DNA strands, but only 2 have been active. The 97 % of DNA, which humans have been taught is junk, is quite specific in its uses and functions. DNA is what defines you, as it is the code which sets the parameters of your entire existence. Portions of your genetics are manifested, and expressed, while other portions have been shut off, and they will become active as the soul grows. Several years ago, Russian scientists began finding multi-strand DNA, yet they did not understand why, or how this came to be. We understand these occurrences as part of the natural process which all species go through, which also fundamentally shapes your perception and reality. And, the changes which are occurring, are affecting all life on this planet.

However, the few interfere with these processes to manipulate Humanities outcome for their greater good. When we look at DNA, its functions, and uses, we must consider all aspects of the whole, including the agenda, what role it plays, and how it is relative to Human growth and outcome. DNA is the central spire to fundamental growth of all life, and many strategies, implored by the agenda, are relative to the intervention of this natural process. Vaccines, GMO's, RFID technology, chem-trails,

etc., are designed to alter, and modify human DNA, in a way which halts, or stunts, this process. This, as a result, shuts down the DNA activation process, and it "dumbs one down," one could say.

Because of this aspect of the agenda, we also look at the terms Apocalypse and Revelation. When we look at the most basic understanding of what these two words mean, we see that Apocalypse is Greek, and it means "discovery of knowledge, or "the lifting of the veil." The word Revelation means to reveal something hidden, or an awakening. This time which humanity faces is a time of growth, not their end. The simplicity of the truth has just been hidden in plain sight. The deception and manipulation utilized by the agenda, is designed in a way where the soul chooses to cause harm to their self. Even if the soul is not entirely aware of the real nature of intent of something which they choose to partake in, they have still chosen to partake of their own free will. Yet, this system is not static. It is quite fluid, and humans are capable of creating the reality they so choose. When souls begin to understand the truth behind what actually exists, they also have the choice to alter these accepted paradigms of reality, in a manner which will heal, and undo the harm which has been caused.

Throughout the histories of many cultures, and the prophetic teachings found around the world, from ancient Egypt,

to the Mayans, and everywhere in between, there was a foretelling of this time which Humanity approaches, and now faces, as they were aware of a natural process which they knew Humanity would grow through. However, there are many false truth systems, and paradigms, which create much fear and separation. And, this is a time of great change, when DNA is becoming active that once was shut off. It is not a time of destruction, but rather a time when the veil will fall away. It is meant to be Humanities awakening from a long slumber.

The growth process is comparable to the visual image of a bulls-eye. Imagine the center dot as your current existence. Each expanding circle is another tier of growth in the dimensional constructs of consciousness. Over time, as each strand becomes active, a new dimensional conscious perception becomes "illuminated," as a candle is always brightest in the darkest of night. And, it is not that we begin to see something new; we just begin to see what was always there, hiding in plain sight. DNA is fundamental to every aspect of your existence, including your thoughts, ideas, and conscious constructs.

The origin of human genetics, is as diverse as the variety of humans which exist on this planet. Human DNA did not come from one place, but rather a collaborative contribution by many, and there are 250+ genomes within the Human genetic code, which are not of terrestrial origin. The Rh- factor is relative to this

tidbit of information. Humans were not created as a slave race, as so many popular ancient alien theorists would have one believe. Humans were created, by many, for the same reasons parents create life here; the legacy which exists beyond the self. When we look at the popular ancient alien theories, and the main stream accepted constructs, we are always lead back to one source, Zechariah Sitchen, the grandfather of it all, one could say. We are bound by our understanding that his translations are not based in truth. They are biased as there is a motif, and there is also a means to the end of his work. He is a human translating something without a full understanding of that which he perceived. Therefore, the translations are reflected through his own constructs of the self, which is not an accurate representation of Humanities most basic accuracy of historical reference.

Whenever souls enter this arena, in the quest for truth, we always advise others to tread cautiously, allowing their truth to reflect the bigger picture. Is it true there are those who manipulate and mislead humanity? Yes, it is. However, that is not the story of their creation. They began from something much greater than any being. They were created out of love. They were created with the same basics needs to love, and be loved. And, anything that humans do, which violates this very basic aspect of the self, is extremely harmful to their very nature as conscious beings. To harm others only ends up harming the self. And, it is a complete

contradiction to harm another, as all is connected.

The Global Consciousness Grid

Souls must be able to perceive the whole image, if they are to understand the human collective experience. Therefore, we must discuss the global consciousness grid, and how it relates to the bigger picture of Humanity. To understand this concept, we will create a base line of understanding, through our unique perspective of understanding, so we may connect the dots, and others may discern truth from within, through their own perceptions and understanding.

If one imagines the global consciousness grid, as the equivalent of the universal creation's version of a global internet super highway, and how all souls connect, and communicate, with one another, it simplifies our understanding of the symbiotic nature of the whole and individual, and the relation of connection to, and within, all things. It is a universal communication super-highway, which all souls have access to. We can now envision, each physical container, regardless of what form, whether it be cat, dog, cow, sheep, pig, human, etc, as a proverbial "server" which connects to this universal internet, thereby connecting all things through Infinite Creator Consciousness and the global grid. How many souls have experienced how one action they did, had a consequence, or an impact, in a manner which was indirect, and seemingly irrelevant at the moment, then came full circle to reveal

itself later, with regard to its true significance? Our guess, is most share this experience. We understand that we see much less, than that which we see, so we always perceive the power of 10. We assess for every one person we interact it, that action will indirectly affect 10 others. Therefore, we are always conscious of our actions.

One could also envision the conscious grid as an FM bandwidth, and each dimensional frequency is a station on the bandwidth. Until recently, collective Humanity has only been tuned into one station on the radio; 3d. They are now beginning to understand that there are more stations, and they are beginning to tune into them. The body is a physical "radio receiver," which allows the essence of "you" to interpret and express those transmissions within the external physical environment. Understanding the relation, and interaction between the human container, and the non-physical environment, is best conveyed through visualization, simile, and metaphor. The mechanism which allows this constant exchange of information, is the connection (nodal) points, within the container, which connect to the nodal points located throughout the globe. Ley lines, grid points, pyramids, and other archaeological features, are also intrinsically intertwined within this system, as all things are connected.

The connection points within the human body, are what we

will refer to as the chakra, or body centers. DNA is integral to this as it is the coding which dictates the parameters of all manifested existence, including that which we may not always be aware of. Each "node" holds a unique frequency. And, as a soul awakens, and gains expanded conscious understanding, this conscious "shift" of energy also affects the physical container, and alters the vibrational frequencies of these centers, which stimulates and activates them. There are more than 7 chakra, as the 8th - 13th chakra directly correlate to the dimensional conscious growth within the 4 and 5d constructs, and higher frequency chakra are relative to higher dimensional constructs of conscious growth.

Pyramids, and other archaeological locations, are the nodal points, for the planet. Ley lines, and grid points, are similar to the human chakra, and meridian, and they are integrally interconnected. Both affect each other, and there are millions of souls, from many races, who are not from here, who have/do exist side by side with Humanity, all with their purpose within the whole. As we are responsible for grid activation, one part of our purpose for being here is activating certain points within the global grid. There are pyramids located across the globe, which is relative to the activation of the global consciousness grid, and is also a factor within the awakening of the human collective consciousness. And, there are many who are responsible for this process.

As each pyramid is coded (within the DNA) to a specific soul, only a coded soul may activate that point on the grid. And, there is more than one soul coded for each location, as backups. This is a fail safe system, which allows natural progression, and growth, within the whole, regardless of the outcome of the individual. Inside each pyramid, there is a multidimensional room. This room is approximately 10 meters cubed, and is made of solid granite, with no entrances, exits, or seams, and they are not accessible within the 3 dimensional construct. Granite is specific because its unique properties are specific to this process. And, in the center of the room, there is a granite pillar which resembles the shape, and dimensions, of a speaking podium. Suspended freely above the center pillar, are two double-terminated crystals, approximately 2 inches in width, by 6-8 inches in length. These crystals radiate a pure light energy wave form, and when a coded soul interacts with the energy frequencies, the grid point is activated, which also affects the collective consciousness.

There are infinite factors, which can be attributed to the whole picture, as there are many universal factors which affect the whole. Energies, frequencies, and dimensional time lines, are relative to the perception of our conscious thoughts (manifested energy wave forms). How energy, and frequency, is manifested, is relative to the dimensional construct. As dimensions increase, so too does the resonant frequency of the manifested physical expression of that conscious dimensional construct. This is why many souls are experiencing the perception of time speeding up. The dimensional constructs alter the physical reality through consciousness. As the frequencies increase, this also affects the state of physical matter. Cymatics is an excellent visual example of this fundamental. For, instance, in one dimension, water holds the frequency of glass. And, even human science states that physical matter isn't really solid. We understand that our perception is relative to our conscious energy and thought patterns. Perceived physical matter is nothing more than particles vibrating at a specific, and unique, resonant frequency, which humans perceive as the specific properties of matter in a "solid" state. However, as energy is the basis of all existence, nothing is truly solid, it is just the relative perception of our conscious constructs.

This example helps better understand why, and how, physical containers become obsolete. Consciousness is instant, and there is no use for the physical aspect of existence in higher dimension constructs. As a soul grows, they begin to understand the nature of controlling ones external perceived existence, through controlling the nature of one's perceived thoughts. Because thoughts are manifested instantly in higher dimensions, all souls are conscious of their thoughts, and actions. We choose to not create negativity, through our conscious perception of what is best for the whole. This is the process humans are beginning to understand. It is the lesson of learning to direct our actions, which set the course of our path, and ultimately dictates the outcome. Therefore, reality is nothing more than a projection of our perception. All external experiences are nothing more than filters, for a soul to discern truth from within, through their own perceptions and experiences.

As all things are connected; the physical (DNA), and non-physical (consciousness) are innately symbiotic. The most simplified aspects of the whole, and individual, consciousness, and how both integrally affect each other, can be observed in two seemingly non-related events, yet are integrally interwoven in their affect upon the whole. When most souls hear Princess Diana's Death, and 9/11, mentioned with regard to correlation, there is a disconnect as no "visible" connection exists. However, when we look at the similarities of these two events, the nature of relevance as to their purpose, becomes clear. Both events were seen by billions, both events created immense despair and sadness within the collective consciousness, affecting the many at the individual level, while also altering the course of Humanity through altering the state of collective consciousness. Both events allowed a few souls, to control the many, through manipulation, and false truth. It allowed a few to feed off of an immensely powerful collective energy source. Is the bigger picture of symbiosis beginning to become clear? Is the connection, which has always been hidden in plain sight, beginning to emerge from behind the veil of the unknown. Is the candle, of the aha moment, illuminating a new piece of the puzzle?

However, understanding of the global grid's effect on collective consciousness, with regard to what is happening in the current, and how it is relative to humanity as a whole, can be better understood by what many refer to as the "100th Monkey effect." When a certain percentage of the whole has been awakened, a tipping point, or shift, occurs within the collective conscious. A process takes place which affects the collective conscious, thereby activating the remaining whole. And, every thought creates an impact. This is also why one should always be a good steward of their thoughts, and that which they project within the whole. What we think affects our manifested reality, no more so, than upon the self. Ideas become thoughts, thoughts become words, words become actions, actions becomes habits, and habits become who we are and that which we do.

By controlling the energy of the collective conscious, the few are able to do what they do, while Humanity allows it. Those who manipulate the agenda, understand that the heart, and brain, are very powerful electric/magnetic transmitters, and receivers. The heart emits electrical frequencies, which are hundreds of times more powerful than the brain. The heart also emits magnetic frequencies, which are thousands of times more powerful than the brain. That which we "feel", and express, from the heart, through the unique expressions of emotions, has an immense impact on our external environment, just as we are affected by all things within our environment. This may help bring greater understanding to the proverbial understanding that love is the greatest force (energy) in existence. This is also why there is nothing more powerful, than a mother's love. It is the truest aspect of the symbiotic nature of the whole and individual. Dr. Emoto's Water Molecule Experiment is a marvelous example of this fundamental.

The Early Years

The early years, of our existence here, is an aspect of our truth, which is fundamental to our entire perception of understanding, in many ways. As we are a conscious collective back home, we have access to all of our memories through our incarnation. As we have grown, we have continued to "see" our existence, through the eyes of the child within. Growing up here, and living with humans, as a human, was extremely difficult for us. We were the proverbial "black sheep," as we were like no other member of our human family.

The lessons we learned, from the humans we knew as "parents," were exactly that which we did not want to be. The humans we were raised by were cruel and condescending, as loving encouragement was not found in our childhood home. We always felt isolated, as it was made clear by our siblings that we "were not welcome." We found the world, at large, to be cruel and hurtful, and we knew this was not where we were from. What we saw here went against every "truth" we "felt" within as a child, and we did not understand why we were here. Many days, we cried as a child, because we felt homesick, but for a place we could not see. Around the age of 6, we were visited by our family from "home."

We remember the experience well, as it is a moment we

have always been able to return to, whenever we needed a gentle hand hold to make it through the challenges. We grew up on a fully operational 76 acre farm, in the mid-western United States, and we remember rising above our bed, and soaring outside above our home. The sky was clear, the moon was full, and the stars were infinite in their numbers. We could feel no physical sensations, such as temperature, as we were not in our container. We were several hundred feet above our property, floating weightlessly in the night sky above our childhood home. We accepted our experience, and the understanding of who was there became clear. We could see the square patches of crop fields, the horses in the pasture, the cows in their grazing pens, and the lakes reflecting the moonlight like black twinkling pearls. It was absolute harmony.

We desperately asked to be taken home, and it was gently made clear to us, that we must stay because of our purpose. We were devastated, and for decades, until our shift, we did not understand why. After our shift, this experience became clear in its hindsight relevance, as it was part of the long term understanding of remembering who we are, and understanding our truth has always been within.

Through the years, we have always found comfort in the natural world, as it understood us in a way no human ever could. The bees are always busy serving their purpose with a friendly nature, dragonflies always have lots to say, horses understand wisdom very well, cows are friendly and peaceful, dogs are loyal and loving absolute, and cats are always up for causing some mischief and a good laugh, as they are happy fun souls. Nature always provided for us, and protected us from the "storm," as it was our haven from a world we saw as hurtful and not true. Being young, we did not understand how true those basics within us, would become, as time passed, and wisdom clarified the childlike nature of truth. We began to understand that truth is innate within all souls, as it is something which has always been within us. As a child, the systems here could not remove those truths, no matter how hard it tried. We would not give up who we are, and we would not sell our virtues for the material.

We always understood that everything we needed to know, during our time here, we learned as a child: share our toys with others, play nice, ask when we have a question, honesty is the best policy, say please and thank you, be polite and respect others, don't do to others what you don't want done to you... the relative proverbs are endless. Yet, these are the fundamentals that we all understand. What we had a difficult time understanding, in our early years, was that adults would pound these very beliefs into us as a child, yet adults did anything but. They acted selfishly, would tell us as a child we didn't know what we were talking about, and adults have a miraculous ability to perceive an all-knowing status, as they think they know everything, are entitled, and they will fight over the silliest things.

As a child, no one ever listened to us, even when we had something to say, because in their perception, the size of our container, deemed us not "worthy" of their attention. How do adults expect a child to understand the lesson when the action contradicts the word? As a child, we saw how creativity was discouraged, and just shutting up, and doing what we were told, was what seemed to be praised. Not questioning authority was rewarded, and we could never conform to this construct. We faced a harsh tongue lashing, and were called a "smart mouth," on more than one occasion. The human we grew up with, and called father, was a narcissist in the textbook definition. He was extremely controlling, and all forms of abuse were fair game if he was questioned. And, we now understand those lessons for the unlimited patience and understanding which they offer.

It took us many years to gain the patience, understanding, and self control, which we resonate, and radiate, today, as we were an angry bundle of rage as a child. We were mad at the world. But, we slowly understood that every experience is a "test," to see how we respond. Therefore, do we allow our emotions to control us, or do we focus to gain understanding over the energetic frequencies we understand as our emotions? And, this took nothing more than diligent reflection of all things through our self. We always ask our self, if the shoe was on the other foot, or if we were the outsider looking in, how would we perceive the same experience. It just takes focus, and the want to self reflect, no more, no less. It was a journey which forced us to face the most dangerous of adversaries. We had to face our self. And, many things we did not like, which we saw, as our truth required our accountability to face what we saw. Our shift was the catalyst that brought all understanding full circle. It was coming back to the self where the whole became understood.

As with all other experiences, we understood these lessons over time, as understanding of our self, and how we allow the external to affect us. Our "father" never could break us. All he ever managed to do was make us stronger, every time his rage surfaced. Hate, and downright determination, is an amazing motivator, and armor, like nothing else. The will to overcome, and destroy, that which causes us hurt, is far stronger than any soul who suffers enough to cause harm upon us, or others.

And, when we became a parent, and understood the cycle, we understood that evil truly begets evil, and how we defeated the cycle of hate was with love. We didn't change the system. We changed what we did to achieve the desired results we were wanting all along. How we changed our reality was from within, through that which we did. We embraced the darkest energy of hate, absorbed it, transferred it into an energy we could use, and reflected it as a source of strength and determination. All souls hold that dark place within, with purpose, and we must understand the beast within, to understand the beauty of its existence. This is understanding the self, for all which we are.

As we became a mom, and the understanding, of the cycle of life, came full circle; we understood our experiences, and why we went through the traumas, trials, tribulations, and hardships. The day we became a mom, we understood our children would never know an existence of cruelty, and hurt, as we had known. They would never know an existence of oppression and have-nots. They would never know a hard life and told to just "deal with it." What they would know was an existence of truth, where they would be able to exist as the sovereign beings which they are, where living in truth of self was the standard by which their upbringing would be set.

We saw that we, then and there, broke the cycle of hate with love. We understood that the change was truly a direct result of our actions, not our words. It is living our truth where the greatest understanding of self is attained, as experience is life's greatest teacher. We never forgot how we saw the world, through our child eyes, and we always reflected from this perspective through every interaction with our children. It is the symbiotic universality of the whole and individual.

Education vs. Intelligence

Setting the framework of understanding, and wisdom, within a soul, requires a careful balance between education and intelligence. Many souls associate these terms as interchangeable, when they are actually symbiotic. As they are different, one should neither be confused, nor exchanged, with the other. When we break these two words down, and what they represent in their most basic understanding, it clarifies many blurred lines, as we are then able to understand their overall use, purpose, and function, so we may understand how best to apply these fundamentals, by reflecting them through the self. This in turn allows a very unique course, which is optimal for each soul, so they may achieve the greatest level of growth.

We understand education as the forefront specifics, and details, by which the parameters of our manifested existence is defined. Intelligence is the hindsight understanding of the spaces between the specifics, and details, to discern the understanding of what is defined in the education. Intelligence is understanding the how's and why's of "the what's", education is knowing "the what's."

Education is learning the five "W's," while intelligence is indeed the understanding within the spaces of the "W's." Education is learned in the forefront, whereas intelligence is understood in hindsight. One could say education is the literal aspect of perceived reality, whereas intelligence is the proverbial aspect. The five W's can be metaphorically observed as pieces to a puzzle. Every piece is a part of education, but when the pieces work together in ubiquitous harmony, as the individual is necessary to the whole and vice versus, intelligence is the glue which brings the whole image of understanding into focus.

      The most common question humans ask is, "What is the purpose of life?" When we look at purpose, we look at the commonalities which every soul experiences. And learning is one of those universal constants within all things. If there is one part of our purpose, which holds the greatest impact, above all other aspects, it is when we impart our complete wisdom and understanding, with others, so they may grow, and expand, while the continuation of life, and the legacy, thrives long after we have departed.

      As the purpose of existence is to learn, so to does this make the topic of education, and intelligence, imperative to the foundation of all experiences, and existence. And, if we perceive Earth as a place where many souls come to learn, through this life time, by gaining understanding through experience, which is lived and perceived, like the "schools" we see here, it is the intelligence gained in hindsight, which deems the greatest educational value. How do we allow the experience to affect us, and what do we choose to learn from it?

There are infinite lessons, with educational value, yet it is the wisdom, and understanding, which is gained in hindsight. There are many lessons which have educated us with regard to understanding our place in the whole. Souls are taught here, that what they perceive is how things are everywhere. Yet, how many souls have traveled abroad, to understand the perspective of being "the outsider looking in?" How many souls truly open their self up to diversity, as opposed to criticizing that which does not conform to their preconceived notions, and programmed beliefs? How does shutting one's self off, from all which existence has to offer, educate a soul? It doesn't.

In 2004, we became the "outsider" looking in. We have always lived in the United States, yet for a week, we became the "alien," once again, when we traveled abroad to visit Europe. Now, the specifics, and details, as to the purpose of our trip, are irrelevant. It is the hindsight wisdom, and understanding, of the experience which is relevant to our journey. We visited, London, Paris, Belgium, Amsterdam, and a brief view of Dover and Calais, because we crossed the English Channel by Hovercraft. A discovery which was quite the surprise, was seeing an Aldi's in Calais. Being a "country bumpkin" from the mid-west, we were surprised at how such an elegant, and culturally wealthy country, had the same store which was 5 minutes from our childhood home. It was a culture shock, to say the least, and its significance would not have been perceived by any other, the way we perceived this Aha! Moment.

To be the outsider is a unique experience which offers a vast treasure trove of infinite wisdom and understanding. To truly see that the way things are in places, is quite different than what we think we know, is a very humbling, and compassionate, experience. To see that souls are truly no different on the inside, regardless of the external differences, brings the simplicity of truth into much clearer focus. It was the truest, most basic, reflection of a "diverse" understanding, and how we are just one part in a much greater whole. It was the obvious beautiful intelligent design of diversity, which became so abundantly clear.

An excellent exercise which better demonstrates this lesson is to imagine you are standing at the cross walk in a major downtown center, with skyscrapers towering above. As you stand on the sidewalk, and observe your surroundings, you see the typical sights; street lights, cars, buildings, pedestrians. Now, let us observe our surroundings from the 30th floor of that same building which you are standing next too. Now, what do we see? We see skylines and the entire city. The people now appear as ants, scurrying about insignificantly in their daily existence. We see the horizon, which is not visible from the ground, as the buildings are blocking the view. Now, do we actually see anything "different" from these two view points, or are we just seeing the same thing, from two very unique perspectives?

European's were fascinated by us, not because we are "cool" or "special," in any way (however completely eccentric, and adorable, with a touch of "bratty" we are), but rather because we live an hour away from Disney World. This little "human" curiosity intrigued us most endearingly, as it was an immediate reflection of similar differences, because we immediately thought of our "Aldi's experience." We found it intriguing that a location held such high regard for how others shaped their perception of us. It was an educational experience, which provided the hindsight intelligence, that was the greatest lesson of remembering that what we see is not always the way things are, and ego is irrelevant to whole of truth. The world, would get very strange with a whole bunch of "me's" running around.

There are no limits, to what a soul is able to achieve, except for the limits which we place upon the self. Whenever most souls are faced with a challenge, they will usually talk their self out of ever trying, before any others ever have a chance to do so. Humans commonly refer to this as a self defeating attitude. It is just a construct which has become accepted within the collective conscious, therefore it is expressed and manifested.

Education, here, teaches children the "cant's" of everything. It creates the labels and constructs which shape, and mold, the paradigms of young minds. It creates the compartmentalization of existence, to the limitations of a 3 dimensional existence, not accounting for any other aspects of the self. From day one, souls here, and those who came before them, are taught to believe exactly as those who hide behind the mechanisms of human oligarchy desire, for the benefit of a few souls, through a very deceptive perception. Souls are taught to place their trust in all external authorities, while being taught to ignore the internal authority of the self. When was the last time you placed your trust in "you," and truly believed in your self, above all else?

Humans are taught that learning is something temporary which they do, and one can fail if they don't do as they are told vs. learning being the collaborative understanding of existence, which is part of who we are? It is a never ending process, with infinite variables, and flexibility, where failure does not exist in the face of perseverance. How does one "fail" at gaining understanding? To us, there is no pass, or fail, in truth. In truth, there is only gaining understanding. It is a process which is creative by its very nature, as it is a collaborative continuous exchange between the whole and the individual.

Through the years we have come to understand the fluid nature of learning, and mistakes are part of those lessons. Mistakes are criticized, and condemned here, which creates separation, and division. It creates a competitive, and combative, environment, which creates distortions, and distractions, in the most basic understandings of truth. We understand mistakes as learning tools, and they are embraced for the wisdom, and guidance, which they offer. Mistakes are never criticized back home, as they are used as a reflection for hindsight understanding.

Over the years, we have come to understand the truest nature of what education is here, from our first hand experiences as a parent. It has never been focused on teaching children how to think, but rather teaching them what to think. And, we never agreed with this construct as it always conflicted within the environment which we raised our children at home. Our home was always based in the understanding that every experience offers a lesson. Creativity is encouraged, living in truth is highly rewarded, and questioning everything is the gold standard of learning. Human education contradicted this entire.

We have faced many battles, with the public education system, which resulted in our choice to remove both of our children, from public education, and enroll them in home school. Our daughter was a sophomore in high school, when we removed her, because the environment was such that her peers were the catalyst for self-destructive behavior. Education was not the primary focus in public high school; popularity, immorality, and self-centered behavior based in instant gratification was rewarded.

Our son's removal came one year later, after the final battle of many, which was the proverbial straw which broke the camel's back. Removing them, in hindsight, was the best decision we ever made in their best interest as sovereign beings.

Our son is similar to us, in many ways, when we were his age. He was always a quiet shy child who was very introverted. Opening up to others was not something he did. As he has grown, however, we cannot say this is relative. Like us, he is now a confident chatter bug, because his environment is not oppressive, but rather encouraging of self expression. As part of our journey, our son was enrolled in a public elementary school, which employed specialists who work with Pre-K children. He was 3 years old when he began school, because of issues which resulted from vaccinations when he was a baby. And, on his first day, his backpack was bigger than he was, it seemed. The first two years, we could not have been happier. The school he attended through Pre-K, and Kindergarten, was amazing, as the staff was very professional, quite skilled, and our son excelled.

Then, his first grade year approached, and we were required to switch schools, to his home school, because he no longer needed the programs they offered. He was our super-champ and overcame many obstacles like the trooper he is. We began to see changes in his behavior, after a couple of months into the new school year, at his new school. He shut down, one day, and would no longer speak, or interact, with us, when we were on school grounds. He would keep his head down, and the first two days we thought he just "wanted to be home", on the third day we knew something was wrong. We had a "feeling" about his teacher being mean to the children, but we had no "proof," just a hunch. So, we decided to acquire proof of our energy reads, as we never react out of assumption. We must have first hand information to support our action. The next day, we slipped an audio recorder into our son's bag, and let it record the entire day. That afternoon, we picked our son up like usual, as he was a car rider and did not ride the bus.

We grabbed the recorder and pressed play, and what we heard appalled us. We heard psychological, and verbal abuse, that no one should endure. We immediately went to the principal and played the tape. We let the teacher's own words bury her. We said, switch him to another class, and fire the teacher, or we report the school to the media. The principal asked for an emailed copy of the file, with a break down of time stamps, listing the abuses, because we refused to part with the original file. The next day, our son was switched to another teacher, and for the remainder of the year, the teacher he was placed with was a perfect fit, and he blossomed. We learned a valuable lesson from this, and became a very involved classroom parent, as we keep our children close, and our watchful concerns even closer.

The first half of his second grade year was fairly

uneventful, except for our move from our first home, to where we currently reside. However, the second half was not so harmonious. We picked our son up from school, one day, and he began to cry, very distraught. We were quite bothered by this, as this was not usual behavior, and we asked him what was wrong. Our son told us that he had said that our sun would supernova one day, to a few other children in his class. And, when the teacher asked him who said that, and he told her it was us, his teacher told him that we lied. This devastated him, and we were not pleased. However, we decided to ask the teacher, the following morning, to explain what had happened. We were hoping it was just a misunderstanding. What we discovered was far worse than what we had imagined.

     The next morning, upon asking the teacher to elaborate the previous days events, she said, "Yes, I told him what you said was a lie, as I didn't want it to scare the other kids." We blew our top. Honesty, respect, integrity, and truth, are the central tenets, and foundation, in our home, and we will not hesitate to take down anyone that attempts to undermine our family values and structure. And "now" we had the very system, which we had entrusted him to, creating conflict within our home, by causing negativity to our son. The situation did not transpire well, and as a result, we had our son switched to a new school. The staff had attempted to intimidate us with the police officer on duty, while we were at school the following day, and we were not biting. We had gone in to apologize, for blowing our top in front of the students. Yet, we were also expecting an apology to our son, for what had been caused in our home. The teacher refused to apologize, we put our foot down, the principal brought the officer in the room, and we politely put the officer in her place, and departed. We went home, and declared war through their superiors. Within days, our son was in a new school, and finished the remainder of the school year rather peacefully.

Then, along comes third grade, the final year where we could no longer tolerate the continuous battles with public schools. Throughout the year, we had been to school on several occasions, because our son was being bullied by staff and students. The final blow came, the week before the last day of school, when our son cried, while we were taking him to school. He told us that he didn't want to go, because they were mean to him, and he was all alone. We could take it no more, and we had warned the school during our previous visit, if it wasn't resolved, there would be hell to pay, and head's would roll. The bully would become the bullied, as our children are off limits.

We dropped him off, immediately went home and called his daddy, explained the situation, and we were told, "Go do what you do best." We returned immediately to pick up our son. We were still in our pajamas, as it was 8:30 in the morning, and we work from home. We didn't care about our appearance, because

137

we weren't there to win friends and influence people. We were there to take our son home, for good, and we were willing to mow down anyone in our path. As mom, no one harms our offspring.

We entered the office, stated clearly we were picking our son up, taking him home, and blew our top regarding the incompetence of the staff and their inability to resolve the issue. The secretary proceeded to stand up, insulted us by calling us a welfare mom, because we were in our pajamas, and that was her worst mistake. Attempting to bully us, when we were there for bullying, was a very bad choice of action. We were unable to walk away, as we were waiting for our son, and we destroyed her false truths without mercy. We made it clear, exactly where she stood, by pointing to our company truck, and letting her know that we own it (we are the boss), and she was a slave, who should be quiet and return to doing exactly what her master told her to do. As soon as our son emerged, we immediately left. The staff was furious, and we found it hilarious.

About 30 minutes later, out of nowhere, an ear-shattering rap on the front door breaks the peaceful quiet of our home. It was an attempt of intimidation at its finest, but it only triggered our hunting mode. We go into full seek and destroy mode when threatened, especially when we are at home. The school sent an officer to our home, to hand deliver a letter, which should have been mailed, or not sent at all. We had made it clear ,before we left the school grounds, we would not be returning, ever. The letter the officer handed us stated that if we ever returned on school property again, we would go to jail. As we understood this was nothing more than a "principal on a power trip" we gave the officer an earful. In short, we explained what happened, told the cop he was trespassing, not welcome, and he better never return to our property. We also told him, to tell that bitch principal, that if she had anything to say, she could drive to our house and say it in person. Once the cop left, the issue had subsided.

As a result, we chose home school, and this is our second year. Our son excels at learning, in a way "public" education could not offer, as we are able to guide his lessons in ways which are best suited to his methods of learning. He never did well in a public school setting, because he is not an auditory lecture learner. Our son excels with tactile, and visual, learning through the hands on first hand experience of doing, not watching. He is true to his Sirian soul traits, just like his "daddy", who is also his hero and best friend. His daddy is who he learns through best, as they are two drops in the same ocean. They are the same consciousness, which has chosen to experience a double existence. They are mirror images of each other. In hindsight, we understand that what we perceive as education, and intelligence, are not interchangeable, and removing our children from the system, was the best choice we ever made in their best interest of self growth.

Emotions

Understanding human emotion, is an integral aspect of the soul understanding the self. Going back briefly, to the topic of communication, we can correlate this as an aspect of unspoken communication. Energy, and frequencies, do not just exist in the physical, chemical, magnetic, and electrical forms which humans have become accustomed to. Energy is the basis of all existence. And, gaining understanding in the infinite forms energy takes, is similar to learning a new language. Emotions are nothing more than unique energy frequencies, which are emitted throughout the environment, and the human container is the receiver, by which the soul interprets, and manifests those energies into an expressed emotion. It is the process of manifesting conscious energy into physical 3 dimensional reality. Each emotional energy has a unique signature, or frequency, and it is how a person chooses to perceive the energy which ultimately affects how it is expressed; anger, sadness, happiness, etc. Emotion is the final manifested expression of those energy frequencies.

When it comes to understanding the self, there are very basic strategies, one can implore, to better interpret, and understand what it is they are truly perceiving. The hindsight understanding we share, is based on first hand real time experience, and having gone through this process also, we understand them well. As part of our purpose is to assist others where, and when, we are able; sharing our experiences, and understanding, in a very intimate way, is part of that purpose. Because our home is quite different in many ways, we must live exactly as humans, as one cannot offer assistance without a frame of reference. We also understand that our time here, will assist others, as they choose to interact with Humanity throughout their growth. Many of our lessons will serve no relevance to us, but will be immensely relative to others in hindsight.

We also understand that the whole and individual are symbiotic, and one does not exist without the other. And, when we reflect upon our experiences, it is always from the internal perspective of the self in relation to the whole. Interacting with an infinite number of souls, over the past few years, since we began speaking openly with humans in January 2013, has offered greater understanding about the self, than any other lesson. As every experience offers a lesson, so to does every interaction we experience with others.

Over time, we began to understand, that it was not what others did, which truly mattered. It was how we allowed those experiences, and interactions, to affect us which mattered most. As all experiences are temporary, what will we be able to say of our actions in hindsight? Regardless of what others may do, or how they may choose to be, we will always maintain our truth to never lose our humanity, and uphold our care/compassion for others. As it is our truth to live, the consequences for not living our truth are also ours to live in accountability of the self.

Whenever we interact with another soul, we do not focus on the container which we see with our human eyes. We focus on the energy of the soul within. We do not listen to what others say, we watch what they do. A soul will tell us everything we need to know, without ever saying a word. Most souls don't realize they tell others exactly what they wish to convey, whether they are aware this communication is taking place, or not. If a soul is causing harm, we understand that all pain, whether it is anger, sadness, rage, meanness, etc. comes from a place of hurt, even if the source of that pain is not so obvious.

Happy souls don't create harm upon others, because they are happy. Therefore, they are not so concerned with what others do. What good does it do to hurt the hurt? This seems rather redundant, and illogical, to us. In many cases, just letting a soul vent the negative energy, is all it really takes to tear down walls and build bridges. Most souls lash out, because it is how they "cry for help," so others will hear their plea, in a way, which protects the self, in a false truth construct. If we had a dollar for every soul who was hurtful to us, we could have bought the Rothschild's off long ago. In the beginning, we questioned every aspect of why a soul would do what they do. And, in some cases, it would take us days to respond to the harshest comments. Now, these interactions have become second nature, and our responses are instantaneous. We have put our self through every baseline human experience, and there is nothing which will throw us off of our path of truth. We have been incinerated in the fires of truth, and the steel of our truth was also forged by those same fires. Because of this, our foundation is unbreakable; we know our self above all else.

We have placed our self directly in the path of conflict, as it was necessary in the learning process of gaining understanding from the human perspective. Over time, we were able to catalog, and discern, what those energies, and experiences, truly meant at their most basic levels of understanding. In the search for truth, we reflected upon each experience, with regard to how the external experience affected our perception of truth within. Why did the action make us feel the way we felt? Over time, we began to see our self as the calm center, or the eye of the hurricane. The swirling winds, and surrounding chaos, were every external experience, and filter, we perceived within our existence. We perceive our self as the calm center, and we guide the path of the storm.

What we have come to understand, over time, is that a soul truly does not affect who are, unless we allow them to do so. And, we have learned much more from others, than we could ever impart during our time here, as we are always the teacher, and the student. The lesson of the whole and individual being symbiotic becomes very apparent in every aspect of our existence. Once we see the connection within all things, and the ripple effect of action, it is impossible to un-see it. The universal truths, which are innate within all things, become as clear as the nose on our face. And, this lesson also applies to the agenda.

The few can only do to humans, that which humans allow. If they did not tolerate the hurt, it would not exist. Always remember that the only thing we truly have control over is the self. And, it doesn't matter what happens at the end of the day, it is how we allow the experience to affect us which truly matters. As one begins to understand the self, they also begin to understand that control comes from within. And, when souls live their truth, without fear, oppression, guilt, or shame, they once again begin to regain the control within their existence. Living one's truth is exactly how one defeats the agenda. It is the Universal Game of Polarity Integration. Once the simple truth is revealed, this image becomes much easier to see as the fog evaporates from the morning landscape.

Health and Well-Being

As we have discussed in other topics, many factors are imperative to the overall, and optimal, health and well-being of any soul. There are many "non-physical" factors, along with the physical aspects, which affect human containers, and humans are beginning to understand this. Consciousness, energy, food, the environment, big pharma, and other factors, interact with each other, and affect the overall health of an individual. The "placebo affect" is a recognized, and accepted, fundamental in modern medicine, yet humans still dismiss this construct, for the basic truths which exist within the understanding. It is the understanding of how the conscious mind holds immense influence over the human container. The human body is capable of being healed of any illness. The body is capable of healing itself, and maintaining optimal balance, when conscious thought is also balanced.

As humans continue their growth, they will eventually gain the understanding of how consciousness affects the physical container. Where we are from, food is not required. Food is also something we do not care about, during our time here. Diet affects the harmonic frequency of the human container, and food intake (eating meat specifically) increases the density. Because we are capable of consciously regulating metabolic function at the cellular level, we only require what is necessary to sustain life functions and balanced frequencies. We eat roughly 2-3 meals per week, and we do not consume life. Eating meat is not something we do, as we see souls within all forms of containers.

We touch on the topic of meat consumption, because humans were taught to be meat eaters. By design, they are vegetarians. Now, it is not a mortal sin, to "consume meat", as there are races which do. Some even use the practice to lower their frequencies when they are too elevated, but it is very relevant to how the few hold Humans in a primitive state of consciousness. The less we eat, the lighter we resonate, and the more clear our pathways are. This is why people are taught to eat 3 square meals a day. Focusing on needing food, in consciousness, affects the physical container, thereby also increasing the perceived need to feed. And, this increases soul density and holds one in a physical state of existence with much greater ease. When, in actuality, Humans do not require food intake, at the levels in which they were taught. Humans were taught, "I have to eat regularly."

Humans, with their current sedentary existence, only need 1000-1500 calories per day, yet they intake much more. This is also why studies show fasting holds amazing health benefits when done in a balanced action. As souls grow, over time, the need for food becomes irrelevant, as the container also becomes obsolete.

Back home, we do not experience disease, or illness, of any kind, as physical containers are not required, and the energies and frequencies are balanced. Disease does not exist everywhere. It is the manifested expression of imbalance within existence. Understanding this fundamental contrast in perception, the simplified truth of health, and well-being, becomes clear. Health, and wellness, is a way of being, not a "thing" which one does. The "health", or balance, of a physical container, is directly affected by energy, frequencies, and consciousness. Humans understand this construct as the placebo affect, or mind over matter. It is just how one perceives it which creates the understanding.

The lesson of consciousness affecting health, was truly understood through our human experience of becoming a mom, and the understanding of the truest extension of our self, and our connection to all things. We were always blessed, with our daughter, as like us, she was a child who never suffered illness. Her health could rival any pathogen. However, when our son was born, we were not so fortunate. But, we can say that what we are about to share, are not experiences which we look back upon, with sadness. Quite to the contrary. They are the fire which burned away all false truths, to expose only the most naked of truths within. It was from these fires, were we became unbreakable. It is a foundation which is indestructible, as our experiences speak a much louder truth, than any words a soul could ever speak.

For someone to tell us what our truth is, is completely illogical. We know who we are. We understand souls reflect upon others, exactly that which they see in their self. Therefore, we also understand that what they do reveals who they are, and no other. What someone does, does not reflect upon us, it reflects upon them. We are not afraid to take any soul on, because we live our truth. And, we hold no fear for what we perceive with our five human senses. We always understood that a piece of paper, and a white lab coat, do not denote intelligence, wisdom and understanding do. A piece of "educated" paper does not make one "smart," wisdom and understanding do. We have never met a doctor, lawyer, merchant, or chief, who's "god complex" successfully stood against truth. Doctors do not like being questioned, yet we do not care. As mom, we are the protector and nurturer of our offspring. We, as mom, nurture, protect, and provide what is in the best interest of our loved ones, and no other. We are not here to stroke some "professional's" ego. We manage their care and choose the path of treatment, as we understand optimal health is not found in big pharma, and the doctors knew their place. They were only their to fulfill needs which we could not. They were only there to assist.

We remember the day, our very unpleasant, and extended, history with the medical system began. It was the summer of 2005, and we were 24 weeks along in our pregnancy. Now, we were never the "glowing" mom-to-be, nor did we ever feel "good" through either of our pregnancies. But, we were very aware of all sensations and energies regarding our biology. The patterns of complications were the same with both of our children. We went into labor at 24 weeks gestation with both of our children. However, with our daughter, we were able to carry through full term. She got quite comfy, settled in, and decided to hang out an extra week. She was a happy butterball, and the best Christmas present we ever got from "Santa." She came home in a stocking, on Christmas Eve Day.

We were admitted to the hospital in early July 2005, when we were pregnant with our son, yet our due date was mid-October. The day we entered the hospital, we had gone to the doctor, because we felt something was wrong. We were airlifted to Tampa General, when our ultrasound showed that our amniotic sac had ruptured, and this was also when the gravity of the situation settled in. We were not leaving until our son was born. Through our inpatient status, over several weeks, awaiting our son's arrival, the medical team made it very clear how we would face every hardship, and our son would likely be "horribly handicapped" in laymen terms. Our living guardian was beside his self. He was being told by the doctors, that all of these potentially devastating outcomes, including our deaths, could be likely outcomes. He was home alone, when not at the hospital, contemplating how bad it could be. We always told him not to worry, as everything would be okay; we told him our son was safe, because we had placed an energy field around him, which would allow his little body to heal and grow. We knew he would be okay, but our other half still worried. The proverbial cliche "love is the most powerful energy in existence," is more true in its simplicity, than many souls realize. It is a simple truth which hides in plain sight.

Our son was born, at 27 weeks (13 weeks premature), after we sat in a hospital bed for three weeks. The day he was born, our son was a fighter, and a trooper, from the start. He was breathing on his own, which surprised the medical team, and they put him on an oxygen c-pap. He was 2 pounds 1.2 ounces, at birth, and he was so small he could fit in a coffee cup. No sooner, than we enter our overnight room, from recovery, as we delivered our son by emergency c-section, the games soon began. Before the anesthesia had time to wear off, some "woman" enters our room, and asks if they can use our son for a study. It doesn't matter what "drug" we are on, we do not lose our conscious sense of direction. The claws and fangs were out. We looked at her coldly, and said, "You will not touch him. He has been through enough, and he will be left in peace to heal and get well."

We ended up basically living at the NICU (neo-natal intensive care unit), while our son was growing before our eyes. The day he was born, his eyes were still sealed shut, and his skin was still transparent. We observed the third trimester of develop, in a way few experience. We spent everyday with our son watching over him closely. And, as time passed, we began to know the staff of the NICU (neo-natal intensive care unit) and gained the respect of the staff. We became as well versed, on the topic of neo-natalogy, as any doctor, and we were always helpful by volunteering an extra set of hands when we were there. We became the resident "mom" one could say. The staff enjoyed our presence, because we kept the doctors in balance. We were not the mom to play "god" with. When it comes to our children, we are god, and we will slam down the ax, with a big ole' lightning bolt of truth, which will humble the biggest ego's. The best interest of our children is our primary concern, not placating the ego of some false truth human in shiny "monkey suit."

Because we are genetically linked, physically, to our offspring, we hold a unique connection with them, which does not apply to any other soul bond, including soul mates. Offspring are the exception. We contribute our DNA to the creation of their container, which is the reason a mom "knows" her children in a way no other ever can, or will. This is also the innate fundamental understanding of energy, frequencies, and consciousness, which has always been the guide of our truth within and has always told us when something is wrong.

We faced many battles, and challenges, but none more complicated, than the human ego. But, one experience, in particular, is of special mention, because it is an experience which has guided us in profound ways, through a truth which runs through the core of who we are; the divine right to protect our life and the life of our offspring. We had requested from the NICU staff, that our son's eyes be covered from the fluorescent lighting, as we had discovered research that implicated the link between fluorescent lightning, and a condition known as ROP (Retinopathy of Prematurity), after being informed that our son had the mildest form. In severe cases, the retina detaches and causes permanent blindness. When we were not at the hospital, we were at home, researching every topic, article, study, and document we could find regarding premature birth and neo-natal medicine. We became a self educated expert. We understood knowledge is power, and we are always well armed for any battle.

On this occasion, the doctor said no to our request. We pushed the issue, and the neo-natalogist told us if we provided evidence, he would consider it. We agreed. We went home and researched everything we could find on the subject. When we went to the hospital the next day; we had printed a 6 inch stack of documents for his review.

When we arrived, we immediately set the stack down, and asked the nurses to get the doctor. He walked up, we repeated our request, showed him the stack of documents, and stated, "Here is what you requested, now please honor our request." He was not happy. He immediately went on the defensive, and referenced a study which had been done, showing there was no link. However, the doctor did not account for that which he did not see. We read the same study the night before, and two comparative articles which revealed flaws within the control group, which rendered the study invalid. We called him out, in front of his staff, and made him eat his own words. From our peripheral vision, we could see the head's of the nurses, lobbing back and forth, from their boss, to us, as the battle of intelligence vs. ego, raged onward. By the time the dispute was over, the doctor had stormed out, and refused to be present in the NICU when we were there. Imagine the blow to his ego, when a 27 year-old "new mom" crushed his piece of paper, and education, which he held with such high regard. After all his years of "education", and loads of debt, who in this case looked like the dumb-ass? The ego always makes the greatest speech we will ever regret. He should not have misplaced his trust in the external. From that day on, we held unlimited respect within the staff. This experience was the ultimate lesson of understanding that we should never misplace our trust in the external. Our trust should always be placed within.

As the years passed, and our son became a toddler. He was a happy baby which was curious and inquisitive. He was in his 2's, when we learned the truth, of many things we did not like. We were always against vaccines, but every external influence, stated otherwise. We never agreed with vaccines, as it just felt wrong to us to put something in the body which was not meant to be. It was never based on anything other than an internal "feeling." Our daughter was vaccinated in her younger years, with no side effects. But, with our son, being older, and wiser, we were more staunchly against vaccines with our son, because the feeling of "wrongness" had intensified.

We were told by our pediatrician, that our son would not be allowed to attend school without them. We were never made aware, that personal exemptions even existed. We discovered this after our son's final series of shots, after the damage had been done. We acquired the exemption, the day after we discovered the information, and they have been vaccine free for more than 8 years. We did not like it, but we were still under the veil of 3d, and many things we did not see. The vaccinations ended years before our shift began, but we begrudgingly consented, and felt horrible for doing so, for some time, in hindsight. It was our actions to undo the harm caused, which also eased our hurt. We channeled those "emotional" energies into a healthy form which produced the desired results. For many years, we were angry with our self, for allowing what had happened, but we understood that living to destroy the hurt, is exactly what healed it.

Our son was always sick (we mean almost hospital bound sick) after he would receive his vaccinations, which we were told were harmless side effects. And, then, his two-year shots were given, and everything literally changed "overnight." Within 24 hours, he had stopped everything... talking, playing, being curious... everything. What once was an aware conscious being behind those beautiful brown eyes, suddenly were empty caverns of nothingness. We were furious. We immediately knew it was the vaccines. As mom, we had no doubts what we "knew," and any doctor who stood in our way, was perceived as making a personal declaration of war. We said he would never be touched by vaccinations again, and this began a war which would not end until what we had allowed, had been healed. For months, we lived, ate, and breathed, the search for truth, until the light began to shine.

Our pediatrician sent us to a hospital, where they specialize in autistic children, but we knew our son wasn't autistic. We understood he was suffering side effects of being poisoned by vaccines, but at that time, we knew nothing of the actual ingredients, or "real truths" behind the agenda of vaccines. We just understood that he had been poisoned by a foreign body which had been introduced into his system. The doctor we spoke with that day, had already decided our son's "autistic" outcome, and only asked leading questions which confirmed her diagnosis. She wanted to test his chromosomes, and we laughed at her. We told her it wasn't autism, as the symptoms we were seeing, were similar to certain physical sensitivities we have. She didn't care, as her ego had blinded her. In her eyes, being a doctor meant always being right. To us, it is the ultimate hypocrisy of the Hippocratic Oath. We said the appointment was a waste of our time, and we called our doctor to immediately get a second opinion. He referred us to a specialist who worked with sensory disorders.

We fell in love on the first visit. They diagnosed him within 5 minutes, by observing his non-physical communication, as having "Tactile Hypersensitivity Disorder." This is when the nervous system is highly sensitive, the sense of touch is amplified, and it creates a sensory overload in the nervous system. For us, touching wet/cold items makes us very cranky. They were able to describe his symptoms, with precision accuracy, which was congruent with our first hand experiences, and they spent months working with our son, in a way which provided his needs so he could heal and overcome the side effects of the vaccines. And, we can say diet was imperative to this detoxification process. Fruits, vegetable, nuts, and whole grains were the key, otherwise known as food, not food "products."

Our children have been vaccine free, since then, and through years of hard work, we were able to undo the hurt, which the system caused. How we did that was by living our truth, regardless of the doubt, and criticism, which we faced from others. Now, our son is 10 years old, and perfectly healthy. He is fully aware and an amazingly inquisitive soul.

Discipline and Justice

All souls innately know "right from wrong." Some just choose to listen to the little voice within, and some do not. We understand the constructs of "discipline," and "justice," from an alternate, and unique, perspective of understanding of the perceived reality, here. Yet, the basic fundamentals of truth are universal to all souls, regardless of our perceived paradigms, beliefs, and constructs. We understand that religion is the "framework" by which all parameters, pertaining to what is "acceptable" discipline and justice, are set. And, when we understand that obedience, and fear, are instilled, so a few can control the many, it brings into much more clear focus, the simple truth of the bigger picture.

Where we are from, it is a strict violation of universal law, to create harm, or negativity, of any kind, upon another. However, as no soul is perfect, we will make mistakes in this process, and it is the eventual understanding of our similarities, which allow us to overcome our differences. Yet, even though a soul is free to choose their action, the universal paradox applies, which states we are not free of the consequence of the action, per rules of the universal law of karma.

Back home, punishment is not a construct which exists, as it does here. Where we are from, all mistakes are guided in wisdom and understanding. All souls make mistakes, and if we wish to judge another, we must do so through the self. We may only expect from others, that which we expect from the self. The lesson of consequence must always be congruent with the action. And, a lesson must also be applicable to both the administrator, and their charge. What is the lesson which is to be learned, so wiser choices may be executed in future actions, so mistakes are not repeated.

We are never allowed to seek personal action in hindsight, as to create harm upon another violates everything we exist for. We exist to save life, not destroy it. We may only prevent, and stop, the action which causes the hurt, in the current. We cannot undo what has been done, as evil only begets evil. Revenge and retaliation are false truth, as they do not teach lessons. They are manifested reactions to the energies humans interpret as emotions, it is not the assessment of logic. It is based in the "me" instead of the "we."

We may never take a life, however balance is the key to existence. If a soul stands in truest defense of life, when no other option is logical to outcome of well-being, and stopping the action will not stop continued harm, trading the life of the soul which causes hurt, to protect the life of a soul who does not, is acceptable, and no karmic action will be enacted in consequence. Per rules of universal law, a soul is accountable for their actions, and a soul must face the consequence of said action. Put simply, the golden rule is a universal constant which applies to all interactions. We are to treat others exactly how we wish to be treated.

Tough love is a concept well known, but few understand its truest universality. Tough love is the ability to let go of control, over that which we have no control over. It is the understanding that all souls must walk their path, and they are also responsible for the consequence. Whenever we must address a mistake, we always approach with understanding that it is not our place to harm others. It is only our place to stop the action which causes hurt. It is our purpose to teach others, not punish them. No soul is perfect, therefore, no soul has a right to judge another. We may only assess the action in question.

No soul holds the "right" to decide the life, or death, of another, as these are parameters, set by existence, with symmetry to the natural progression of soul growth. This applies to all souls, regardless of the container. Euthanasia is murder wrapped in a pleasant labeled construct of acceptance. Even the experience of birth, and death, is fundamental to a soul's growth. A disruption in this process, disrupts the soul growth. Those who cause hurt, should be healed, not harmed, and many lessons can be most harsh indeed. Those who reap financial gains, while others starve at their expense, should be required to give ALL their material possessions to those who need it most. Those who take a life, should be confined to an existence which requires them to save life. A soul who steals, not out of basic need, but for selfish gain, should work for those they stole from, in equality with the goods stolen. As with any mistake, a lesson should always accompany the action.

The Mom Perspective

While at the store one day, placing bags in our car, we were witness to an event, in which one of our cardinal rules, respect, had been severely violated. Our attention had been drawn to a woman, who was proceeding to yell at one of the employees. She didn't like where he had been collecting carts and stacking them, and proceeded to insult, and belittle, the employee, with no cause for the action. As we watched this older woman proceed to treat this employee most harshly, who was also a younger man, we could not stand by idly, as we are not built to tolerate that which causes hurt. We spoke up and said, "Wow!" Everyone stopped and looked in our direction. We proceeded to speak, "Where did you learn to be so angry?" She responded, in a rather startled stutter, "Well, I was just telling him how..." We interrupted, stating, "No, you weren't just telling him anything. You are back-lashing. He wasn't doing anything wrong. You are just miserable and wanted something to complain about it, because misery loves company." We continued with this digression of behavior, and continued... "The reason you did what you did, is because he is an employee, and you know he won't respond. You are a bully. However, as a customer, we can respond however we wish. You know, people should just be nicer to each other, and what you have done is truly pathetic." She looked at us, most offended, and said, "Well, I never..." And, we interjected by stating, "Oh, yes, we just did, and you don't like it. Go be miserable somewhere else, as no one wants to hear it." And, then, we walked away. The employee approached us, as we went to enter our vehicle to leave, and he told us, "Thank you." We said, "anytime," and smiled in response.

As we drove away, it was a fabulous experience to reflect upon, because if souls merely extended common respect for one another, the world would be a very different, and much more simple existence to navigate. If everyone became tired of the behavior, and merely refused to tolerate it, it would not exist. And, we reflect upon this in relation to the cycle of life, because our children are a constant reminder of how our actions create a ripple effect which affects the whole of existence. When we look at children, we easily see that they are not born into this world to hate, they are not born prejudice, they are not born to be anyway but exactly who they are, as we are taught everything we think we know as adults. When we reflect our selves from the perspective of our children, we understand that they have truly taught us as much about life, as we have taught them. They are the living proverb which brings complete understanding full circle. There are infinite lessons of wisdom, and living breathing proverbs, which we experience through our legacy, procreation, and the cycle of life.

We are the mom, who did not have a mom, to seek advice

from. We ended up taking the crash course, and hit every branch, on the ugly mistake tree of life, possible. As parenting is not a perfect science, with plenty of room for error, we always remember that we are no more perfect than the mistakes of our offspring. Our children are a perfect reflection of our mistakes. As our children have grown, we reflect, in hindsight, on the lessons of wisdom being a parent has offered, and what it means, to be a parent, in its most basic fundamental truth.

We find our self asking the very basic question, "What does it mean to be a parent?" If we break this down to its most basic truth, a parent is one who nurtures, guides, and protects their young, while imparting all of their wisdom and understanding, so the legacy may continue and thrive independently. We always understood our children were not "ours." They did not belong to us. They were their own conscious beings. They were placed in our care, and it was our duty to be a good steward in the best interest of their well being, and optimal growth, during their time here. It was never our place to tell them who they are. To quote a famous movie line, "mother is the nameful god on the lips, and in the hearts, of all children."

Through the eyes of a child, a parent is a god. There is nothing a parent can't do, fix, or heal. They know everything, and can do anything. They are the invincible hero which makes any "monster", whether in the closet, or under the bed, flee with all their might. A parent is the physical manifested expression of what children see as "godlike." And, it is our responsibility to uphold that truth through the honor, and integrity, of our actions. Children do not listen to what we say, they imitate what we do. Children are the greatest mirror of truth. They have not yet been conditioned to forget to see truth, as what happens to adults through the years of programming, and indoctrination, even from those we entrust with our best interest, namely mom and dad.

As a child, it was common place in our home, for favoritism to be given to our siblings, and we were the fifth wheel which just had to accept it. Equality was absent apparent, in our childhood home, especially to the youngest eyes. When we became the parent, we remembered how we perceived our existence as a child, and it has always been how we set the parameters for all interactions with others.

When others ask us who we are, our typical response is, "We are mom." That is because that is not what, but "who" we are. As a mom, it is our purpose to nurture, guide, and protect others, and this is inclusive of all souls. When we interact with other souls we perceive our interactions through the eyes of a mom, regardless of the container we see before us. The details, and specifics, of what we see with our human eyes holds no relevance to the truth of who we are interacting with, which is a conscious being. All souls have the same basic needs, and when we interact with other souls, not as a combatant in the game of "Who is right," but, rather just perceive, and accept, that individual as the conscious being which they are, it removes the bias of programmed false truth, to give way to unfiltered unbiased truth from within. When souls are not so busy having to defend their self, it is amazing what others have to offer, which we do not. No soul can do everything, That is why every soul has a purpose, so everything can get done.

It is one of the lessons of balance, or knowing how to choose our battles wisely. We see things in a very simple way, with regard to what we deem as relevant, or not. We have always viewed things from the long game perspective, and if it will have no impact on our existence a year from now, is it worth expending our energy on it? Is it worth getting upset over? In our home, we have always held moral virtues as the pinnacle of our home, not conformity to a system. We always entrusted honesty, respect, trust, loyalty, honor, integrity, morality, accountability, and truth, as the standards, above all else in our home. Honesty is never disciplined, no matter how much we disagree with the action. We always understood that our children did not do what we say, they did what we did. We can only expect from them, that which we expect from our self. We never taught them to conform. We taught them to be exactly who they are, no more, no less.

The construct of "punishment", as humans understand it,

does not exist in our home. All matters, within our home, are resolved through hindsight wisdom and understanding, and this includes actions which correct the mistake. Mistakes have always been understood for the lessons of wisdom they offer, and when a mistake is made, we do not criticize, or condemn the soul, we connect the dots, and explain the bigger picture, so they may understand the lesson, for that which it offers, so they do not choose to repeat the action. Have our children tested the boundaries? Of course, just as all young souls do. And, like with humans, children get into all sorts of trouble. However, youth has its advantages, as older souls understand youth is where mistakes are made. In order for one to become old and wise, they must first be young and dumb. Life is lived forward, yet it is understood backwards. As a parent, we owe it to our children to impart what we have learned with them, so they may understand the hindsight, in the forefront. As insanity is hereditary, and we get it from our children, if there is one thing we have learned above all else, it is unlimited patience, and to always be serious, but never take anything too seriously. Nothing screams "patience" like a hungry baby at 2:00 am, after a week of no sleep.

It is not our purpose to just provide their needs. It is our purpose to provide the best existence possible, and in every way, which encourages their growth of self. Wisdom, is a wealth which no amount of money can buy. It is an infinite fountain of resources from which they will be able to drink. It is a well which will never run dry. But, we also understand, that while we have been not only their guides, and teachers, we are also their greatest students. Being a mom, our children have taught us more about life, than we could ever teach them, as they are a living, unbiased, and neutral reflection of the self. We see in them exactly that which we are. With our children, we see all the best that is within us. They are a living extension of who we are. Therefore, it would be counterproductive to not nurture those connections with all which we are.

Because they are our checks, and balances, there is also a special trigger, which is only triggered by our offspring. Their presence shuts down any aggression, with exception only to defending life. They are the very heart of our being, and we are responsible for guiding the path which allows them to shape who they are. We set the stage by which their conscious constructs are developed. What is the legacy we wish to impart, once our time has passed, and we return home. What will be able to say for our actions in hindsight? How will our legacy be remembered? As we must live the outcome of our choice, what is the course we choose for our self? And, we impart this lesson with our children also.

When it comes to action and consequence, all matters of guidance are reflected through the understanding of cause and effect. If our children make a mistake, they are responsible for holding the self accountable for the action, and taking the appropriate steps to harmonize what once was imbalanced. They will ultimately live with the results of their choices, not us. Therefore, it is not our place to make their choices for them. It is our place to guide them well, through hindsight wisdom, and understanding, based on first hand experience, so they may wisely choose their actions for the self.

As our children have grown, our oldest is now 18. Like us, she faced many traumas and hardships, because of a man she called "father," who cared only for his self even at the expense of his flesh-and-blood's well-being. After years of many challenges, and rebellion, we can say that she has chosen her path well. She, like many teenagers, screamed for what we could no longer provide to her, independence and true freedom. We had removed her from public school, a year before, because the environment had become quite destructive to her well-being and growth as an individual. She despised it, and refused to continue. She wanted freedom, but we could not let go of the years of hardship, and buckling down on her, which we had done.

All children come with their own personalized manual, neatly tucked away within. We as parents only need open the manual and read it. And, every child has their own unique needs. Our son is very different, in many ways, yet similar in others, from his sister. Understanding they both are their own soul, and each has their own unique needs, we cannot say we raised them the same way, yet they sit equally in the game of life. It is just how they choose their path, and the needs required for that, which are different. However, the basic need to love, and be loved, is innate, and necessary, for all souls. It is the core of how they grow and find their way, in truth.

Our rules have always simple, live your truth to its fullest, by doing, and the world will be your playground, with our support and blessing. Waste your talents, do nothing, and be lazy, and mom will put the motivation boots on. Because we, as a mom, had also been conditioned by years of behaviors, we understood what our daughter needed, was not much different than what we, or any other soul, needed, but we could no longer offer. She needed to live her life, for her, without our intervention. And, we gave it to her as much as we did not want to. She went to live with her grandmother, became employed (she was promoted to manager after only 3 months), is financially responsible, mature, lives on her own, and continues to grow, and expand, every day. We could not be more "mama bear" proud of her.

We speak regularly, as we are now two peas in a pod, and we are best friends. She laughs with us now, about how all of the things we told her, when she was younger, now begin to make sense. The only thing she doesn't understand, is how, we as mom, know everything, and we are always one step ahead? We chuckle when this topic comes up, and we always tell her, "One day, when you are a mom, you will understand." She laughs because of the cryptic nature of the statement, and understands that one day it will make sense. It is not that we are capable of seeing something she does not. The understanding within this statement, is just the simple understanding that if we reflect our experiences, through the eyes of our children, we begin to see that they are the cycle coming full circle. If we know what we would have done, it is not difficult to understand what they will do. We always joke with her, because she is just as feisty, and ornery, as we are. She keeps us on our toes, and holds us to truth, as we have always done with her. But, as any parent understands, we will always hold the upper hand, as we will always hold more experience. Where do our children think their attitudes come from? As mom, we hold much greater experience at being a stubborn "asshole."

We have always been the judge, jury, and executioner, in our home. However, our home has always been one of equal voice. We are never unwilling to listen to our children, when they have something to say. However, if they wish to argue, they better be able to present a valid argument in front of the court, and the verdict will be decided. Reasonable requests are always granted, as we encourage self growth, and understanding. We encourage them to explore their path freely, and we are always close by, safely watching from a healthy distance. As tough love is part of growth, boo-boo's and ouchie's are par for the course.

However, there are certain lines, which are clearly drawn, and they are not negotiable. To cause harm, upon another, is strictly forbidden in our home, and is met with the most humbling of lessons. There was an occasion, when our daughter was about 12. This was a time of great rebellion, when she thought her britches were bigger than they actually were. Our children have always been taught very simple rules. If you choose to take a step against another, be prepared for whatever comes back in return. Quite simply, do not EVER take the first swing. If you do, be prepared to get hit back.

On this particular day, our daughter became angry when we took her phone, because of behaviors we discovered, which were quite damaging to the optimal growth of her well-being. She was furious. She demanded her phone, and when we didn't return it, she became livid. We made it very clear, because she would not walk away, if she proceeded forward, we would put her on the ground. She didn't listen, as most feisty rebellious teenagers do not. We grabbed her, put her on the ground, and held her there while we giggled. That's it, nothing more. We cracked up because she was completely furious, and the only one who was mad was her. We told her, "Whenever you are done fighting, we will let you up, and "when" that is will be decided by you, because you are only fighting with your self." As soon as we were finished, she paused, looked at us, saw we were smiling at her, most lovingly (seeing that the lesson was sinking in) and she stopped. She immediately understood the lesson, and we let her up. Never again did she stand against us. And, to this day, we still laugh about that day, as she reflects back upon her experiences. When it came to our daughter, the apple didn't fall next to the tree, she hit the tree.

Family Matters

The topic of family, and relationships, will receive a varying degree of responses, based within the perceptions of the experiences of the individual. Many souls, when asked, will relate to positive experiences, while others may recall negative, or unpleasant, experiences. However, all souls relate to the proverbial truths hidden within the spaces, as any soul has a "family story" which is relative to who they are, and why they are the way they are. Because our home is quite different, with regard to the family structure, we have a very unique perception.

Back home, families do not exist, as they do here. As we are a conscious collective, souls are not "born," they have grown to the appropriate dimensional construct of conscious understanding, and they have chosen to expand their experiences by connecting with the whole. Souls, who are new to our home, are welcomed with open arms. There is always a teacher, or guide, available, to assist with understanding. It is comparable to one having access to the Library of Congress, with a tutor available for any subject, and nothing is off limits.

We do not perceive the individual, with regard to the construct of relationships/family, we only see the whole of outcome. If something affects one, it affects, all. Action is not isolated, just as it is not isolated here. Humans have just been taught to perceive their self, as separate, or outside, of the whole, when, in contrast, they are beginning to understand the whole is part of everything, and they are a part of that whole. We do not choose to separate our self, through exclusion of the "me." We perceive our self inclusively withing the "we." To us, they are one in the same. These fundamentals also apply with human families and relationships.

In reflection of our "relationship," with our living guardian of more than 14 years, what we understand in the current, is much more expanded, and all encompassing, than what we perceived so long ago, in the beginning of our interactions. We have truly come to understand the greatest principles of Sun-Tzu, and the Art of War, and balance. We have never read the book, which he left behind, because there is no need. As he is part of our collective, we have access to his collective wisdom, as he is one of our greatest teachers. If one wishes to "know" the outcome of any battle, his teachings will always predict the outcome. There is no greater teacher than conflict and compromise. So, how does one bring hindsight understanding, to the forefront of experience? Through reflection of the self. And, when we look back, we can say that we are exactly where we are supposed to be, and we now see that even back then, we always knew where we would end up. However, we can also state that how we arrived at our past's "future outcome," and the path which was taken, was in no way something we could have foreseen.

Our living guardian is true to the Sirian way, and loyalty is held above all else. Betrayal is unforgivable, and trust is not given, it is earned. Being Lyran, we are loving, kind, and trusting. These contrasts of character created many conflicts over time, as we have hurt each other, more than any two souls could hurt each other, yet these were necessary lessons. Regardless of what has happened, we have always stood by each other. Nothing is unforgivable, we will never walk away from each other, and we know each other better than any other. These lessons strengthened us like no other lesson could. His harshness strengthened our soft edges, while our compassion has smoothed his rough surface. We have balanced each other through understanding that peace does not mean no conflict, it means overcoming conflict through understanding what we are in reality, which is a same fraternity of conscious beings. We are two parts of the same whole. And, in the end, it is counterproductive to hurt another, as in the end, it only hurts the self to do so.

Because life holds infinite variables, one must understand where they are headed, yet one must always be flexible in their course of action, as we never know the path which lay in between. When we met our living guardian, so many years ago (we were both from St. Louis), but he was on vacation, and visiting from Florida, where he lived. We did not put much attention into him initially, as he was not the usual "character" we were drawn to. As we began to interact, we began to share commonalities of lifetime experiences, which drew us together like moths to a flame. We enjoyed conversation, and there was always something to say. We were so intimately connected in consciousness, the physical did not matter to either of us. We had a blast eating pancakes, at the pancake house at 2:00 am, while drinking coffee, and falling asleep cuddling, talking about our entire existence.

Every embarrassing moment, which could happen to us, in front of each other, occurred, in the beginning. We rear-ended him on his motorcycle, he choked us out horse-playing one day, he passed out at the movie theater after driving over 1000 miles to see us (he thinks he's superman with an impervious cape... ego blow central), jacked up on a pot of coffee and no sleep, we have run into a glass door at full speed; laughing right along with everyone else in the house, and we have knocked our self out while getting into his car, by hitting our head on the door. But, these are the little moments, that we reflect upon, which hold the greatest value. No one else will ever be able to laugh at those moments. No one else will ever share that history. No one else will share the moments, we remember, of our children growing through the years. No one else held our hand, while we sat in the hospital during the time our son was born. No one else will ever be able to sit in that chair.

Over time, we began to understand that we were the truest harmonious chaos of polar opposites. We were the perfect blend of fire and ice. Our perceptions of the bigger picture, and those constructs which truly mattered, were a dead match. However, how we would choose to reach our destination, regardless of where, could not be more different. If we choose left, he will always choose right. And, we have always been this way. But, looking back, we understand the conflicts have always been necessary for our growth. He is our wisest teacher, most curious student, greatest adversary, harshest critic, favorite supporter, devil's advocate, and best friend, as we are to him. He challenges us in a way, which no other soul will ever do. We understood "who" he was the day he pushed the button no other could. It was a button designed only for him. He is the only soul who can make us angry, upset, eternally joyous, and have the impact which he has upon us. We have come to understand that the reason he can cause a reaction in us like no other, is because we only get upset over that which we truly care about. We would not get upset if we didn't care.

Over time, who we are is not possible to understand, in totality, without him, as he is part of our existence. It would not be the way it is, today, without him. After 14+ years of being partners, in every way (we even work together), we know no existence without him. Even now, as we write this collective understanding, he is the backbone of what we do. His support, allows us the infinite resources we need to live our purpose. He is one half to our whole. He is the silent partner, and he completes us absolute. The fundamental human construct of family, and relationships, has taught us the lesson of the art of balance, and learning to choose our battles wisely.

These lessons became most clear, through the time of our shift. Part of understanding our truth, was in the perception, and understanding of our external experiences. Because we are polar opposites, he is always a few years ahead of us in understanding the 3 dimensional existence, while we are always a few years ahead, in the understanding of universal existence. Because he was not awake through our shift, he was our greatest critic, and we received much grief. But, it was not without cause. Because our nature is to be open, and loving, we have indirectly placed our self in a position which questioned his loyalty, more than once. We understood, in hindsight, our actions were not in truth, or they would have created no negativity, even though our intent was honest, and true. The indirect action caused hurt, which is not allowed. He made us question our self, in every way possible, yet these lessons were necessary in our understanding, and his also. However, because he was present for our entire shift, it was also part of his truth. And, about a year after we began speaking with humans openly, he went through his shift. Our experiences were imperative to the understanding of his experiences through reflection of discernment. He no longer questioned our truth, because he had now experienced it first hand, in a way no words could ever convey.

It is the lesson of give and take, it is the lesson of compromise. It was the ultimate lesson in understanding the Universal Game. It is the lesson of understanding that duality truly does not exist. Good and bad are truly relative to the perception of the individual experience. Because the heart, and brain, are electromagnetic transmitters, we have learned the entire communication system of each other, through the energies and frequencies of the soul. Other than the mundane tasks of daily 3 dimensional existence, words are completely irrelevant to our understanding of each other. We know exactly what the other is thinking, and doing, before they do. We compliment each other in every way. We do not struggle for "control." We understand our purposes. We respect and honor him, for the protector, and provider which he is, and we are honored as the nurturer and guide, which we are. We are each others' greatest adversary, and supporter. Between us, there is nothing we can't do, as together, we are complete.

The Money Game

Finances, and economics, at the individual level of perception, hold a very basic understanding of simplicity, when it is broken down to it's most fundamental purpose, and meaning. When we understand that economics is nothing more than the exchange of goods available, we understand that supply is relative to demand. It is the balance of not spending more than one has. The reason this topic is so relative to the collective understanding, is because debt is a primary method of enslavement, which the agenda uses to trap souls, through the perceived understanding that they are "drowning in debt" one could say. If we have no debt, the system has no control, as we are not obligated to others. But, how does one accomplish this?

Through our childhood, we grew up in a very impoverished home. The humans we grew up with, were poor in every way. They lacked, finances, education, intelligence, open-mindedness, or tolerance. As a result, they were never able to teach us anything of real value, either. Everything we have come to understand, has been through our experiences, and we always saw money as something everyone else had, but it was not something which ever made us happy. What made us happy was what we could have been provided, but weren't. We wanted wise loving guides; what we were shown was the harshest truths existence had to offer.

Through our early adult years, we were never very good with money, but we were never horrible. Our crucial flaw was the inability to hold a "job," as we hated the enslavement. Money was never the issue for us. However, when we met our other half, he was very money oriented. He was able to pinch a dollar, out of a penny, in ways that amazed us. He spoke the language of business, and money, in a way which we speak wisdom and understanding. Because we never cared much for money, we were happy to allow him to be the primary financial mindset. We always believed in being well informed, but control was not an issue which created conflict. We happily allowed him to be our guide, and teacher. And, over the years, we have learned well. Now, we are very aware of how finances, and economics work, on a very efficient, and easily understandable foundation. Anyone can accomplish freedom, and they don't need a million to succeed, as the system has one believe.

Money is only a tool, as it is not what creates success. And, as we progress through this topic, the hindsight understanding will become clear. Through the years, we always heard the "get rich quick" scheme, or the guru selling their book on "make $xxx in xxx days through our secret strategy," or better yet, those amazing pyramid schemes we all here so much about. When it comes down to the most basic simple truths, there are no secrets, or magic tricks; it is just simplifying economics and finances to their most basic aspects of purpose and function.

Money is the first thing which comes to mind, for most people, when the topic of economics, or finances, is approached. However, we see money as just one aspect of the bigger picture. Money is just a conduit, by which a few souls manipulate, and deceive, others by creating the perceived value of a material item, when said value truly does not exist, except within the conscious construct of those who perceive it as valuable. The "money" system was created as a system designed to control the many. Paper money, or currency, which holds no tangible value of equal trade (paper for paper) is a concept which is unique to this planet, as economic systems are unique to each civilization. This is obvious even on this planet, as one can see how many monetary "economic systems" which exist here.

However, instead of souls accepting money, as the tool, and resource, which it is, to make the most of their existence, in ways which truly nurture the soul; humans are instead taught that "money" is the "status" by which success is measured. Success, and wealth, are not measured by money, as those with money can, and do, testify. When money is of no concern, souls truly begin to perceive what is of real value. But, no one is ever taught "how" to achieve this.

The system is designed to enslave the many, so a few may

benefit and live well. However, in contrast, when a civilization exists in truth, all souls benefit and live well. The system here teaches us to go to school, be a good student, get rewarded for doing what you're told, get a degree, go to work and make others wealthy. And, hopefully, after the peppy years are over, and we are too tired to explore, because the system spent decades beating us in a slave cubicle, it becomes easy to understand how the many never see the path, yet it lay right in front of them the whole time. The speed and inundation of modern life, just keeps most souls too busy, and distracted, to stop and see things as they are. It is the reason the world moves at lightning speed. When was the last time people just rested and contemplated about their existence?

We never lived above our means, as we understood the simple concept that we must earn, or bring, more resources into our home, than we put out, or consume. Yes, we acquired debt, through the typical big life purchases... buying a home, cars, credit cards, etc. But, no matter how responsibly we saved, or spent, it seemed that every time we would make progress with one step ahead, the system was always there to knock us two steps back. No matter how honest, or "hard working" we were, nothing seemed to unlock that missing "secret" that only the few seemed to know, and never share. After living the "dream" of acquiring the material possessions (house, car, etc.), and a bunch of debt with it, we truly saw that was not what made us happy. It was also not what we truly measured success by. We saw success as freedom. Time is one resource money cannot buy "more" of. The time to do what makes us happy, which a "job" never allowed, because there was always someone telling us our schedule, and when to report to our masters, which dug at the deepest aspects of our truth. We despised everything the system said we should be. The idea of living in a cubicle for many decades, was a far slower, and more painful death, than any criticism, or rejection, the system could throw at us.

We remember the fateful day, which set the wheels in motion, which altered the course of our path, in a way which also dictated our entire outcome. However, at the time, we did not perceive the relevance, or priority, of the experience, at that time. In 2008, we were a night auditor/front desk manager for a major flag (which is also known as the brand) hotel. Because we enjoyed our job, and were awesome sauce at what we did, the "boss" abused our efforts by overworking us. We had become so exhausted, it created the catalyst which set our truth on fire.

Our son was a toddler, through this time; our living guardian worked days, we worked nights (because our son could not be in daycare), and we had run our self into exhaustion, because rest was minimal. On this particular day, we were waiting for our living guardian to arrive home, so we could sleep, and at the time, there was an above ground pool in our backyard.

Because, our sleep was so manipulated, we forgot to remove the ladder. An hour later, we awoke to the loudest "yell-fest" we had ever experienced. We were jarred from our sleep like "fatman" and "little boy" had just arrived.

Our other half came home, to find our son, who was two and a half, at the back door walking outside, because we had passed out, while trying to put him down for a nap. The instant gravity of the potential tragedy, which could have taken place, had our other half not come home when he did, hit us like we had just been driven over by a WWII Sherman Tank. We were devastated. We sat quietly, while our other half vented his anger. We then quietly grabbed our keys, and drove to the beach, a few miles from our home. We sat there, for hours, and cried because the totality of the experience, and everything we saw, came crashing down around us.

While sitting there, overlooking the ocean, and seeing the infinite scope of existence, the pieces began to make sense. However, any hate which we had for the system, had become a cold calculating methodical plan, with no mercy, and no deadline. The entire system, which affected our existence, had just declared war. The moment the system directly affected the safety, and well-being, of our loved ones, was the moment it became a battle to the "death." But, what broke our heart most of all was that ultimately, in the end, it was our choices which lead to the experience. We allowed the system to dictate our actions, and where we placed our loyalties. We struggled with knowing we were scheduled to show up that night, yet we still had not slept, and our rage was clouding our ability to think clearly. All we could see was that we wanted to crush, and destroy, the system which had caused so much pain.

As we sat there, contemplating the lessons of what we had just witnessed, we did not know how we would free our self. How the answer came was in no way anyone could have foretold. But, our focus had erased any fear the system once had upon us. To us, we had nothing left to lose, and everything to gain. We returned home, and went to sleep, feeling horrible from the immense weight, and pressure, of truth beating like a drum, while we accepted that we were living the lie of programming and conformity. The disappointment of self was like a vacuum, sucking the very essence out of who we were. How would we set the example of living in truth, and real freedom, if we could not achieve this for our self. In short, we felt like a complete failure.

As usual, our alarm went off at 10:00 pm, which always gave us an hour to get ready and arrive at work. We didn't budge. We couldn't. Everything in us had frozen, and we could no longer live the way our entire external existence said we were supposed to. We broke. We just began to cry, completely exhausted, and told our other half we had no strength to physically get out of bed. He told us to quit, stay home, and we would figure it out. Those words were all we needed to hear. He called our boss, told her we quit, and we slept like Sleeping Beauty. We were so consumed by our next move, and how we would make things okay, it was the only thing we thought about. Then, about a week passed, and we got the call which catalyzed our experience on that fateful day the week before.

   During the first week of January, 2009, our other half received a phone call, from an associate of his boss' (who also happened to be the owner). This individual informed our other half, that in two weeks, he would not be receiving a paycheck, because his boss had lost his primary method of revenue, and he could no longer afford his salary, which was $40,000. This was the straw that broke the camels back. Everything we were taught, about following the "safe route," was understood in that moment, that the safe path was never truly safe. For that matter, we saw no path which was guaranteed "safe." All roads hold some risk during travel. It is knowing when to take the calculated risk on one's self, which separates those on the narrow path of truth, from those on the wide path of false truth and conformity. We hated the system enough to do something about it. We were taught, by our entire existence here, to place our trust in all things external, But, we now understand that the successful individual innately places trust in the self. That is all it takes, but what no one is ever shown.

We sat for days, considering our plight, accepting that everything in our existence hung in the balance. We realized the gloves were off and "the box" was getting the ultimate beat down. Then, the lightning bulb went off. The company our other half worked for, was a sales company, and our other half was "THE" service department. He was the only service technician. We sat our other half down, and explained to him, that since he had become a liability to his boss, and he could no longer afford him, why not just offer to take over the service department. As his boss was between a rock, and a hard place; We simply stated, "If he lets you go, he can no longer honor his sales contracts on the service end. However, if he lets you bill the customers, and split the income based on a percentage (an incentive to accept the offer), it relieves his liability, while still honoring his contracts. In return, you keep your income, but over time, you will build customers, because we already know the business model works, and the offer will only apply to current customers, therefore he holds no claim on future business. What you make now is the baseline of your income."

At first, it was so far outside of the box of accepted constructs, he dismissed the idea, and we kept speaking about it anyway. However, after a couple of days, he approached us and asked us to explain our idea once again, so we did. Upon concluding with our idea, he agreed and said "let's do it." We spent the rest of the day planning the strategy, by which the "sales pitch" would be "sold" to his boss. The next day, he did exactly as planned.

He left that morning, around 8:30, and we waited patiently, understanding that everything would work out exactly as it was supposed to, and we already knew his boss would accept the offer, as logic did not suggest otherwise. The phone rang at 10:00 am., and the caller ID on our cell phone lit up. It was a moment, that a soul experiences, maybe once, or twice, in their entire existence here. It is a moment which shapes and defines all which will be. And, in many cases, we do not realize the "moment," until it is gone. But, every soul has had this moment of experience, in one form, or another. It is a moment which shapes the very essence of who we are.

As we answered the phone, we heard a brief (yet what seemed an eternal) pause. And, then, the rupture of energy behind the sounds of the words, erupting from his vocal chords, came to life. "I'm free! Oh my god, Boo! He took the offer! Oh my god! I can't believe I am free!" he exclaimed. "I cannot believe it is 10 in the morning, and I am on my way home... A FREE MAN! I am now in control of my income, and no one will ever be able to tell me what I can make. I get to dictate my schedule..." The sentiments flowed, and we quietly listened. We could not have been happier that his freedom had been achieved. And, we immediately set our focus on our next target, which was that nasty little pest called debt. It was time to cut the chain from our neck. The war would not be over, until the system had been completely defeated, and rendered useless. We wanted to be happy, and we would stop at nothing to accomplish this. We also knew the material world was not where we would find it.

Over the next several years, our focus became the elimination of debt. We were tired of seeing the resources, we worked so diligently for, being given away to infinite hands which always seemed to be reaching in our pockets. We couldn't tell souls, what decade it was, the last time we "went out." We do not feel the need to have the latest, and greatest, gadgets, as we do not need to keep up with the Jones'. That was never what made us happy. Now, the Jones' can keep up with us, all day long, if they wish, but that is not what we want. The home we live in, is a direct reflection of what is truly in our best interest. Because, we are always at home, we chose a home which is comfortable and we enjoy. We still go places, of course, and we are not hermits, but everything we "do", regarding activities, is always centered around spending time with our children, and our choices are never public venues. Because we are extremely sensitive to our surroundings, we become exhausted quickly. Our children are always with us, and we wouldn't want it any other way. We are a close family that enjoys being together. We enjoy learning from each other, and our greatest happiness has never been found in the material aspect of our existence.

When we reflect back, upon these experiences, we now understand in hindsight, that what created our truest success, was in no way related to money, finances, or economics; it was simply drive, determination, and focus. Success truly comes from within, and it has always been there. We just choose to sell our self short, when we choose to not apply our self. What we focus on, will always get bigger, because that which we truly seek, we will also be willing to work for, instead of just talking about doing it. No matter what any "success guru" will ever tell you, there is no secret to success. It is simply taking the step of action, and doing. It is not a path which is easy. It is a path which tests us more than any other, and on the days we want to give up the most. It is meant to be difficult, as growth occurs outside of our comfort zones. Everything which we required to succeed, had been there all along; we just never saw it for what it truly was. Everything we needed, was already within us. It just took the right motivation to set the actions into motion.

How Does One Defeat the System

Growing up, we experienced a very impoverished existence, where money was something everyone else had. It was always visible but just out of reach. Through our early adult years, we worked many "jobs." We were always taught the system paradigm of go to school, work hard, go to college, get a good job, buy a house, pay bills, and hopefully retire at the end of a slave life when we could not really enjoy everything life had to offer. We despised the system, because it always felt "wrong" to us. It was not how souls were supposed to exist. It took away from soul growth in a harsh and brutal way. But, as we are older and wiser, we can say what we understood then, was very different from our understanding within the current. It took us many years to understand how to utilize the system to our advantage, to make it work for our well being and best interest. How does one use the system against itself, to undermine it effectively?

We enjoyed being happy, not what the system told us we should want. We never wanted "it." Money was not something we ever truly cared about. We would spend it freely in the pursuit of happiness, and we have always shared our excess with others. The material does not matter to us, as it is temporary, as there is only "so much" any soul truly needs. Where we have gotten in life, was not because of money. Money is just a tool, as it is not what creates the truest measure of success. No matter what we did, to be a "good" person, the system always seemed to be at the ready, to push us two steps back, when we would take a step forward.

The system always seemed designed to destroy people, and hold souls back from growing. But, being young, there were many aspects which we did not see, which we now clearly understand. As life is lived forward, but understood backwards, the hindsight of wisdom becomes truly priceless in the forefront. No one ever taught us "how to beat the system." It was a learning curve where we made many mistakes, but a road where calculated risk was worth the reward. In 2008, we faced a time, like many others, where we were losing two incomes, while having to support a mortgage, debt, and a family. For months, we struggled financially, and did not know what we do. We truly saw that the safe route had never truly been safe. Others dictated our income, free time, family values, etc.

The classic "employee/paycheck" system is a method of control, where others have no say in where their contributions are placed. As a business owner, we hold much greater control regarding "how much" of our work load is contributed to the systems which create hurt on this planet. This is not how living in truth for the self is achieved. It is a bias existence where external influences affect the choices which we ultimately face the consequence for. No one else must face the outcome of our actions. Therefore, they do not hold our greatest well being... or our legacy, at heart, as it is not their heart to hold.

The system is designed to care for the well oiled machine of the whole, while neglecting the symbiotic nature of the individual. We had always been taught, by our entire external influence, that we should place our trust in all external authority. However, we could not place trust anywhere but in our self. We made the choice to quit paying our mortgage, and we were willing to walk away from our first home, because we understood by sacrificing one thing, it would allow us to save all others. We spent many nights, contemplating how best to regain control of our outcome, instead of becoming another long-term statistic. We removed the box entire. We were the "bad" employee, because we never stayed at a job longer than a year. We were criticized by many souls, because we couldn't just "keep a job" and do what we were supposed to. We never cared about what others thought. It wasn't "they" who would make us happy. Being a slave, for someone else' existence was not why we were here. Souls are meant to be more than a "worker bee." We were so angry with the system, we began to live, eat and breathe how to defeat it entire. Now, almost 7 years later, our existence is a much different perception, and understanding. Our home is one of peace and harmony, which is free of the trappings, and deceptions, of the system. Our children have never known a life of hardship. They have always known encouragement through self understanding and their connection to all things within the whole. They have always known an existence free from oppression and enslavement.

As others now may truly see; it was not money which created our reality of success; it was exactly what we chose it to be. We had no excess resources when we chose to change our outcome, as we were broke when we started our company. It was our creativity, drive, focus, and determination which were the foundation. It was understanding that the box truly did not exist, and it was believing in our own capabilities above, and beyond, all else. Souls here are taught to love things and use life. We have always loved life and used things. Living our truth has always been what matters most, not what we can acquire. Souls allow their self to be dictated by the material external existence, because of the perceived value which is placed upon objects. Which, in turn, this is nothing more than the perception of inherent value. Yet, when we truly understand that money is merely relative, and we recognize it for the tool which it is, we understand that attachment to it, is a null and void concept. It doesn't make us who we are. It is just a relative aspect of this lifetime's experiences. Money does not exist everywhere.

There is no simple answer, which anyone will ever impart, as to what path will be best for you. Only you may decide that course. When we hear the financial "experts" and "guru's" speak about the road to success, we hear many "secrets to success" but no secrets rest within. Truth is innate within all souls, because it is ubiquitous as it is universal. It is merely knowing what you are capable of, and being willing to take a calculated risk, to achieve the reward of self growth. This is a path which leads to happiness which also leads to completion of the self. There is no magic trick, or secret formula. It boils down to one simple thing, applying and doing, no more, no less. No one is going to live your existence for you, as no one else is able. It is a path you must walk for your self. It is a path of discomfort, which exists outside of your comfort zones. Yet, once we face a new experience, we understand, in hindsight, that the perceived anticipation, and conscious mindset, was very different than the actual experience. We tend to make challenges bigger than they are. And, most people will talk their self out of something, before anyone else ever has a chance to do so. However, as misery loves company, there is always negative reinforcement available, from the closest of sources. The question then becomes, when we are faced with a challenge, do we become bigger than the challenge, or do we allow the challenge to become bigger than us? Do we focus, or fold?

Creative Ability and the Power of Manifestation

During July, 2015, we were taking a break from our social media, and we were sitting down discussing course of action with our living guardian. Many things came to mind, as being away from everything allowed us clarity to place many things in perspective through a much more clear perspective. We were sitting on our back patio, overlooking our back yard, and we expressed we wanted to create a garden. We wanted to purchase land, because there were many more things we wanted to do, and while speaking with our living guardian, he suggested that we chop down some of the overgrowth in our back yard, to make space. We have been in this house, more than 4 years, and never once had we thought to make room in the backyard, by chopping down the overgrowth. The light bulb went off, and we instantly realized that what we were seeking sat right in front of us. When he gave us the idea; that is exactly what we did. We grabbed a chain saw, lopper, a few other tools, and got to work. And, this is where we get into the idea of creative ability and the power of manifestation.

When we hear others speak, we hear a lot of disconnects which make it very difficult for many people to put the pieces of the puzzle together, in a fundamental real-time way, which people can use within their day to day existence. Therefore, we wanted to share our experience, of what we have done, to help others utilize this information to their best advantage. When it comes to manifestation and creation, even though it is different in many places, it is still the same basic concept, and construct, across the board, regardless of which planet, civilization, or soul group one is from. It doesn't matter. Creation, and manifestation, is the same across the board. It is just how one perceives it, interprets it, and applies it.

When we began this project, our yard was covered by a massive overgrown hedge. We simply took the monkey on our back, and the mouse in our pocket, and we put everyone to work. We did not set a time line, and psychologically prepared our self to work until it was completed. What we did was nothing more than physically demanding work, which required unlimited patience. We did as much as we could, each day, to clear the debris, but we were never in a hurry. We continued this process, day after day, when weather and other factors permitted. We looked at the project knowing it would take many months to complete, and we just said every step forward is one step closer to the goal. It was one less step to take. We accepted the time with unlimited patience, because at some point, we understood it would be completed. As we continued through the project, we almost laughed at our self, because we understood that what we had been seeking all along, sat hiding in plain sight the whole time. We just had not opened our eyes to see it. As the project was finished, we reflected on the 4 months it took us to complete it, from beginning to desired projected goal. Now, many may wonder why we chose to not hire contractors, as some may assume it was for financial reasons, others may assume we did it for the ego, and others will have varying assumptions. However, in the most basic aspect of truth, we did it for others. The greatest growth of self is always found in that which we do for others. We created our living garden, in hopes that it will one day feed others. We enjoy eating healthy, and we believe that all others have a right to this same basic need. No soul should ever go hungry. It is self destructive to the species which allows even one to go hungry. The hindsight simplicity of how "easy" it was to create a food source, which will feed many, made the false truths of hunger, and starvation, even more intolerable.

However, there is no greater reward than the end result of a job well done. As something given is not earned, we hold much greater value to something we worked diligently for vs. something we were handed. The completion of self is met through the challenges we face, as growth is achieved outside of our comfort zones. When we reflect in hindsight, about what the experience taught us, we saw the simplicity of how easy it was to do. The hardest part was the initial psychological preparation. Once we began, the work completed itself. It was nothing more than focusing our energy on what mattered to us, and nothing more. It was consistency, diligence, determination, focus, motivation, and vision of something much greater than our self. And, all of this was found within our self. No one encouraged us, no one cheered us on. It was purely our want, and desire, to create something more, which was the catalyst of manifesting the idea of a garden, into a living tangible reality. We understand that a thousand years ago, modern day mega cities did not exist. They were an idea, not a reality. Today, we see what the will power, and focus, of many ideas, can become when manifested in real time constructs, as a result of the power of creative ability and manifestation. There is no secret, or magic, to the potential of what any soul is capable of. It is just the constructs through which we perceive our existence which set the parameters. You are capable of exactly that which you so choose, as all one needs is to "know" they are truly capable. This is as simple as it gets. Problems, and challenges, will only become as big as we allow them to be. Do we choose to be bigger than the problem, or do we choose to allow the problem to become bigger than the self?

The U.N. Experience

As we continue the hindsight journey, of our lived, and perceived, Human experiences, there was never a lesson of self, more apparent, or relevant, than our two experiences visiting Manhattan, with the intention of introducing our self, at the United Nations, during the general assembly. As we reside near Tampa, this also meant we would be leaving our entire comfort zone, and everything which made us feel safe, as we rarely leave home, and this only enhanced the complexity of our task which lay ahead.

Our first trip, we had been asked, by , to introduce our self, and we were given no further assistance. It was our choice as to how we accomplished this. We had no idea what to do, say, or how to plan the action, and the date of September 23, 2013 was chosen. For this trip, we chose to ride Amtrak, because we had never been on a train, and we wanted the experience. As the months passed, and we spread the message of our plans on social media (we were using Twitter at the time), and many souls expressed they would be there. We had much support, and encouragement, and it ignited a spark within us which was motivating like no other.

The train ride was a scheduled 23 hour trip. We spent much of our time in the dining car, interacting with souls from all walks of life. We enjoyed the experience immensely, as it was a perspective of travel which we rarely see. We saw places which are not view-able by standard vehicles and roadways. Around 3:00 am, as we were making headway, somewhere in Virginia, the train comes to a stop. It was the braking system which stirred us from our slumber, when we sensed the change in velocity. As we sat there, on the tracks, we looked out the window. There was nothing. We were in the middle of nowhere, with nothing but woods as far as the eye could see.

We sat there for hours, not knowing why the train had stopped. Many souls became restless, and irritated, because they were "in a hurry" and had somewhere to be. We just sat there and observed. We understand that there is much more that we do not see, than that which we do. We understood the most basic aspect of truth was that the train would not stop without a reason, even if we did not understand why. By the time the breakfast car had opened, at 6:00 am (3 hours later), people were downright mean. The conductor was passing through our car, one woman stopped him, most rudely, and demanded to know what had happened, and demanded to know why we had been stopped. The conductor politely looked at her, and with a sharp tongue of direct truth, he proceeded to inform the passengers that the reason we had stopped was due to someone stepping onto the tracks, in front of the train ahead of us, as they had chosen to take their life. The reason we were still stopped was due to the fact that crews were still cleaning the scene, and removing what remained of the individual.

As we watched silence fill the car, along with shame and guilt, we just continued to sit in silence. Another hour had passed and we were once again on our way, and we spent the remainder of the trip reflecting on the experience. It was a profound reminder of humble acceptance for that which we do not see. We will never forget the look in that woman's eyes, the moment those words parted the lips of the conductor, and struck the nerve of truth within her, with as much force as the train which took the life of the soul she had disrespected.

There were a couple of souls, which were from New York, and they had warned us to be careful, as New Yorker's can be quite the tough crowd. We politely said thank you, and gave it no more thought. As we arrived at Penn Station, we were exhausted, yet exhilarated. Because we had never been to The Big Apple, we wanted an authentic "New York" experience, and we chose to stay in a flat, in Brooklyn, off the C-line (Shepherd Ave). We had arrived two days early, so we had time to explore the layout, and experience actual times of metro travel, as to get our bearings set. We explored the sights, and found that what we had been told about New Yorker's was quite contrast from our first hand experiences. We could not have been treated more kindly, or friendly, and souls were eager to converse, and very comfortable in their element.

As the days passed, and we shared "tweets" notifying others of our experiences, and continuing to rally the troops, others continued to profess their commitment, and assured us they would be there. On the morning of the "big day," we awoke most uncomfortably. We were far outside of our comfort zones; we could not believe we were in New York, about to walk right up to the UN, with everyone who would be joining us. People were still tweeting as we headed for the subway. We had made our plans clear, and we were to meet everyone at Strawberry Fields at 8:00 am. From there, we would walk right through Manhattan, and straight to the UN.

Upon arriving at Strawberry Fields, we looked at our watch, and saw that we were on time. We looked around, and began to realize, that no one else had shown; not one person. We were jaw-dropped, as we had placed our "faith" in others, because we were perceiving our existence through our self. We were expecting that others would "do" just as we had done. As we stood there, we could not proceed to the U.N., because we were not psychologically prepared for going "alone." We had prepared our self to be with others.

However, as we stood there, after a moment, the realization of the lesson instantly took hold. We began to chuckle, as it all made sense. We placed our trust in the external, instead of where it should have been placed all along, within the self. It was the complete understanding that we must live our truth, above and beyond all else, regardless of the external influences, or what others do. We had been smacked in the face by this lesson, and it is one of the foundations by which we interpret our entire existence today. It is a lesson which sticks out more than most others. Because we were unprepared, for the outcome of events which had transpired, we remained in our flat for the remainder of the trip and reflected upon the experience. Were we upset with those who said they would be there, yet did not show? Of course not. Why would we be upset? It was part of the lesson, of understanding, behind the experience. We still love them dearly regardless.

We were more frustrated that the step from talking, to doing, is such an infinitesimally small step, how does one not take the action of moving forward? Regardless of how long a journey is, if we just continue to take one step forward, and then the next, we will eventually reach the goal. Patience truly becomes dynamic, as impatience becomes static. We were torn, because we knew we had traveled with the purpose of introducing our self, and we had "failed" as far as we were concerned. Yet, the conflict existed within our understanding the lesson. And, knowing all experiences offer a lesson, made the weight of this burden tolerable.

We returned home, and we were very disappointed with

our self for not proceeding with our original purpose. As several months passed, our day to day existence was rather uneventful. Until, the day came once again, and home had sent the request to return once again to the UN. This time, we were prepared to carry this task out, as we had faced the experience once before, and anticipation was subdued. Now, many souls may see this as "outside the box", or just flat out insane, but a soul of truth wears "crazy" as a badge of honor, based within the paradigms of this planet. To us, living exactly who we are is not "outside the box" at all. Quite the contrary. How is being who we are "crazy?" Isn't living a lie of conformity much more insane, considering souls end up working for what they never truly wanted to begin with? How is that sanity? Simply walking up to a soul, and saying hi, and sharing one's experiences is as simple as it gets, to us. It is how people choose to perceive what is shared which creates the complications.

As the months progressed, and we once again scheduled our second trip to the U.N., we were much better prepared. Once again, we shared our intent with others on social media, and the same scenario repeated once again; history of behavior was repeating itself. The day we awoke, September 22, 2014, we were prepared to head to the U.N. regardless of who was with us. Upon arriving at the U.N., we were once again alone. We approached U.N. Security and explained why we were there. When we were asked how many souls were with us, we said none, as we were alone, and we were asked to return when "many" came with us. We politely said okay, and asked, because we had traveled from Tampa for that one day, if anyone would mind if we spent the day "hanging around" while introducing our self to others.

We were told it was not a problem, and we spent the entire day introducing our self to every acronym law enforcement agency/officer, we encountered. We met many interesting individuals, and we received a range of responses from mild criticism to genuine curiosity. Did we expect others to believe our truth? Of course not. It is not every day a human container walks up to someone, and says greetings, we are Feline from Lyra. How are you? Most souls are rather surprised by this. However, because we lovingly accepted the criticism, by merely not retaliating, and simply responding with polite elaborations of wisdom and understanding, these are not experiences which will soon be forgotten by those we encountered. How many years later, and humans not being alone is becoming more widely accepted, will that past experience become relevant to the future "current." In hindsight, those souls will remember the "strange girl" from Lyra, which they met one day in passing. As our actions create infinitely complex ripples throughout the whole, we understand that a seemingly insignificant interaction, within the current experience, may later become obvious as to its truest significance, and impact, upon the whole.

As we returned home from this journey, we did not succeed with introducing our self to the U.N. General Assembly, but we did get a very intimate, and formal, introduction with our self. We understood who we were, so clearly, it revealed the true irrelevance of ego. We understand who we are is exquisite and unique. It is the totality of our qualities which create the whole picture, and many souls share many traits. However, no two souls share all traits. It is the spider web of diversity. All souls have their purpose, and living that purpose is merely truth of self. As we have grown through our experiences, we have come to understand, at the most basic levels, what once filled a space with fear and uncertainty, was slowly replenished with certainty and happiness. We have gained the understanding of perception, that our existence, here, is comparable to a hurricane. The external influences are the winds of chaos which swirl around the eye. We are the eye, the calm center within the chaos, and we guide the storm. It is the truest representation of understanding the self within the whole.

We understood that we were capable of taking the perceived "beast" head, and thrived beyond our comfort zones. The internal prisons, of conscious fear, had been obliterated by our actions through living our truth. We walked right up to the biggest "entity" on the planet, without fear, shame, or hesitation, and smiled with per-ma-grin while we did it. We live exactly who we are, therefore, there is nothing to be afraid of. It was the ultimate test of self, and we came out shining like a new penny. We understood our self, in absolute totality, which allowed the very fires which burnt us, to also create the unbreakable steel which is our truth within. And, any soul is capable of this, they just need to "know" they can. In many cases, it is the self which will talk us out of doing something, before anyone else ever has a chance to intervene.

The Long Game

Every action creates a reaction, and what we do affects the whole, as the ripple effect of action is quite relative to the long game. Therefore, when we look at existence, and outcome, we ask the question, " Where do we wish to be in 5, 10, even 20 years from now?" How do we choose actions, which will manifest the outcome we desire? How do we effectively affect outcome of the whole?

How does one create a long-term conscious construct, and manifest that perceived non-physical thought pattern into a physical tangible reality? Well, when we understand that manifesting a conscious thought is nothing more than focusing our energy into a desired action, which creates the desired outcome, the long game becomes much more simple in understanding. For instance, a thousand years ago, mega-cities like New York City, and Los Angeles, did not exist; they were only a thought. Yet, through many souls, and many generations, the focused collective conscious effort manifested that energy into action, which created the desired outcome. And, in simplicity, Human consciousness did nothing more than utilize the 3 dimensional physical container, to manifest 3d physical results. And, regardless of what path we choose, the most basic aspects of universal truth, which apply to all souls, are also understood by all, as truth is not found in that which we say, it is found in that which we do. And, the long game is where the hindsight of wisdom is understood.

Those who came before us, set the stage for us, just as we will set the stage for our legacy. Humans are taught to look no further than now, without care, or concern, of what will be. They are taught to care only for the self, which creates a blind spot. And, everything here is taught backwards, with the intent of misleading souls, by maintaining the veil of darkness (the absence of understanding). Imagine prophetic texts, throughout history, as nothing more than play books, for the long game, which the few have adhered to for thousands of years. The long game is where they thrive, because to them, it is not about the self, it is about the ultimate outcome of the long game.

Living in truth, and choosing one's path, requires understanding of where one is headed, by understanding where we have been. What is the desired outcome of the action? Why are we doing it, and how is it relative to the bigger picture of outcome, and the long game? Even though it is easy for souls to "imagine" a desirable outcome, or "i wish I had a...," it is the journey which stumps many. However, when we understand the secret to the long game, is that there is no secret, understanding the long game is much more simple in nature.

Because there is much more we do not see, than that which we do, we always account for the unaccounted. We understand that we do not see all, therefore, we always reside on the side of caution. We never assume. Even through our interactions with others, regardless of what others' do, we are always conscious of the long game, and the ripple effect of action. In fall of 2013, we were using Twitter, and we encountered an individual who was not yet awake. Quite to the contrary. He was brutal, harsh, belittling, and down right mean. However, we never lost our compassion, or composure. We continued politely, for days, introspecting as we are doing now, and our communications just ceased. We understood his anger was sourced in his hurt within, because he hated the hurt he saw here.

A few months later, having not heard from this individual; we were contacted. He told us a story of an experience that took place, after our encounter, and everything we had shared made sense all at once. He was a delightful soul who engaged in many insightful conversations thereafter. This experience was also a fundamental lesson in our understanding that what we do now, as insignificant as it may seem, may have profound consequences later. And, we are always conscious of our actions. What will we be able to say for actions in hindsight. Will we stand in truth, or fall in false truth?

Where we are in life, has not been achieved through "instant success", or some magic trick. To us, these constructs are illogical, as there are infinite variables which affect every action.

And, the long game is nothing more than a series of coordinated collaborative interactions, which catalyze a conscious thought into a manifested reality. To us, the long game simplifies down to a few basic fundamentals of innate truth within all souls. In hindsight, a desired outcome is achieved through continued focus of energy, frequencies, and consciousness, which then manifests into a desired outcome.

From a human perspective, it is simply focus, drive, and determination. Many souls, when they undertake a new project, are excited, and put their entire self into the project, and in many cases create exhaustion and burn out. When we understand the subtle mechanisms of what is taking place within the bigger picture, how the long game is relative to the whole becomes clear. The agenda is designed, with the long game as the format for strategy. It utilizes a strategy which keeps humans in the "now." Therefore, Humans do not perceive existence upon a scale of many life times, they perceive an existence of one. They only see what affects them, not others. This construct has contributed to the separation of self, and why humans have a difficult time seeing through the illusions of false truth, so they are able to perceive the whole.

However, when we understand the bigger picture, and our place within the whole, the long game also becomes clear. Whenever we choose a course of action, or deem what relevance an experience has to our existence, we contemplate its relevance to the long game, and how it will affect our existence, and the existence of others, many years from now? Even though we are always serious, we never take anything too seriously. No matter what we experience, we always remember the experience is temporary, whereas existence is eternal. Will what happens truly matter later, and what do we truly seek, as the outcome? But, we never forget that the most seemingly insignificant experiences, to us, can hold a profound affect upon others, even if it is not until in the long game, where this becomes apparent. What we understand is that when we exist in truth, we will be on the right path, even if we do not always see the details of the how's and why's.

Is the Agenda Winning Because of You

When was the last time you were happy? When was the last time you did something good for you? We see so many focused on the agenda. We see many focused on the distractions, fear, and propaganda. Souls choose to live for, and are caught within, the agenda, because they are always worrying about what will happen next. Those who choose to be focused on the agenda, have already allowed the agenda to defeat them, because it consumes their very existence, as what we focus on will always get bigger.

As, we spend our time preparing for what is coming, we feel hard pressed to believe that people do not see that what was, is no longer. Our entire existence has fundamentally changed in a way that will require souls to adapt to a new way of existence. As with all great empires, this time too shall pass. We understand change is a constant fundamental through existence, and we must be flexible, and open to new experiences, if we are to adapt, and thrive, in any given situation. We do not perceive change as a good, or bad, experience. We understand duality is strictly based upon the perception of the individual. What one soul may deem as good, another may deem as bad. We hear much discord within others, as to how they do not like the current systems, yet they rely upon, and fear these very systems failing. When souls are prepared, change is quite manageable, and not something to be feared. Is the idea of change so horrible, when we understand we have always been at the helm regarding our outcome. We may not be able to control the storm, but we can surely adapt to the conditions, to formulate how best to "weather" it. After all, need has always been the father of invention. And, there is nothing to fear, when it comes to change, as it is all relative to the perception. When we hear souls speak about preparation, we hear many souls speak about purchasing guns and weaponry. Be prepared to defend your selves, and fight everyone possible to defend what is yours. But, how many souls are truly thinking in terms of the long game, and on the larger scale, not just the self? We grew up in an era where mom's always had a basement full of daily needs. They just called it being prepared for anything. The idea of "preppers" did not exist. With tradition, we are a mom who carries everything, including the kitchen sink and a spare ambulance, in our purse "just in case." You never know when a band-aid and a kiss are needed for that random boo-boo. We are always willing to help others, and we will care for our neighbors. We are always prepared to provide the basic needs for others, not just our self. When we focus on how best to be prepared for the changes which lay ahead, we are always accounting for the whole. When we look at how the agenda works, we understand that defeating the agenda is not about "prepping." It isn't about locking our self away from others. It is about being able to be the lean-to where others may find comfort, safety, and support. We do not defeat the agenda by taking it head on, we undermine it, one soul at a time. For every soul we assist, it is another brick we remove from the wall, and use to build a bridge.

As a mom, we will always have a hand hold available to others. It is the only way we know. We just hold a very simple understanding that we will only assist others who truly wish to assist the self. If someone does not care enough to work for their own well being, it is not our responsibility to take care of them. It is about souls coming together and pooling their resources for the greater good. Humanity is at a time where they must learn to overcome their selfish greed, by understanding that this home belongs to all, and all are responsible for the whole well-being here.

When we look at the fear, and psychological imprisonment, created here, through the constant distractions, and deceptions, we see the immense stimulus overload of daily existence throughout society as a whole. And, we begin to understand why so many souls have a very difficult time seeing beyond the veil of their limited 3 dimensional constructs. When we truly understand the illusion of paradigms, and beliefs, which are set by what society states is normal, we begin to understand that truth is found within the subtleties, and proverbial meanings, which are hidden within the spaces of the physical 3 dimensional reality, which many perceive using only their 5 human senses.

Whenever a soul engages the agenda, gives it their attention, and focus; they are allowing the agenda to defeat them, because they feed it by supplying it with their time and energy. When we do not focus on the distractions, and rather focus on our existence, and doing that which is beneficial, and allows us to grow, that is how we ultimately overcome the agenda. We understand that learning how to adapt to a system, to best understand how to beat a system, is exactly how we also learn how to utilize the system to our best advantage. We do not allow the external to affect how we manifest, and express, our existence from within. We do not allow negativity, because we do not give it attention. We do not feed the beast.

However, on the occasion, when negativity from the external environment does enter our proximity, we address it, and resolve it, without pause, or hesitation. We never allow a mole hill to become a mountain. But, what constitutes happiness? To us, it is living our truth and purpose. We are happiest when we are being constructive, and productive, in a manner which is beneficial to the greater good. We are restless when we are idle. We begin to feel a sense of frustration when we are not living our purpose to its fullest. The material is not something which matters to us. It is what we cannot buy which creates our greatest wealth. We understand that kindness does not equal weakness, just as aggression does not equal strength. Kindness has always been, and always will be, the greatest strength within. Regardless of what transpires, we always understand that every experience is temporary, and all we are left with is the reflection of what we have done, and what cannot be undone. How we will look back on what we have done? What will we be able to say about our self. Will we be able to stand with honor, or will we hide in the shadows of shame? Happiness is something that only you can decide for you, and it will be unique to the you, and no other. Other souls would not find happiness in our existence, as it is not their purpose to live. Happiness will always be found in that which we do, as something given is not earned. We appreciate what we have worked for much more than that which we are given.

Epilogue

As we conclude our journey together, we would like to impart one final reflection. In hindsight of this competed work, the actuality of the gained understanding through experience, is much less complicated than our perceived anticipation in the forefront. We had originally set the time line of several months, as we have never written a book, or undertaken an experience such as this one. We held no frame of first hand reference to form a base line. We only had what we understood through the external experiences of others.

However, once we began, our pathways opened up, and the words inked their way effortlessly across the pages, which you now see before you. The process of sitting down, at the keyboard, and transferring our non-physical conscious thoughts, into manifested tangible physical form, took nothing more than the focus, drive, and diligent determination. The lesson of patience is understood in the long game, as it is the truest understanding that all things will come to pass, and at some point, we will complete the action. It is the basic understanding within our need to live our truth above all else.

To us, the physical aspect of action was the easy part. A bit time consuming, perhaps, but second nature, and a seamless process, because of our infinite experiences of understanding. It is in the lived, and perceived, experience, where the "labor of love" is best understood. The creation of this project was through infinite experiences, and countless life times. It is a story which was created by the whole, through each individual living their purpose, and truth, in the universal quest of learning, and gaining understanding. We do not see two roses, fighting with each other, on the same bush, over who has prettier petals, just as we have never seen one bee, say to another bee, "That is not "my" problem." We don't see conflict in nature, as it is not innate. What we see is the natural checks and balances within existence. We see the imperfect perfection of harmonious chaos. Then, one must ask, why do humans harm each other? Because it is what they are taught, and nothing more.

As we bid you farewell, we wish to impart a last reminder. In hindsight, as you reflect upon the infinite journey of understanding, which we have traveled together, regardless of what we have shared, what we share is not right, nor wrong, it is merely our perception of understanding. If what we have shared helps you understand "who" you are, in your greatest truth, it has served its purpose.

Therefore, we wish to share a final message, yet this is not our message. It did not originate from us. It was shared by many others, like our self, and as it is independent of us, it is congruent with our truth. Therefore, we wish to transcribe, and share this information, in it's original, and unaltered, format, to add it to this collective understanding, as part of a larger frame of reference. It is a message from many, and whether, or not, you believe our truth, or believe it is a good "story," is irrelevant to us. Truth is what matters.

*A Global Message to Humanity *
(originated 2003: Released 2010)
CHANGE THE WORLD!
"DECIDE WHETHER WE SHOULD SHOW UP!"

Whoever transmitted this translated message to you is irrelevant, and should remain anonymous in your mind. It is what you will do with this message which matters !

Each one of you wishes to exercise her/his free will and experience happiness.

These are attributes that were shown to us and to which we now have access. Your free will depends upon the knowledge you have of your own power. Your happiness depends upon the love that you give and receive.

Like all conscious races at this stage of progress, you may feel isolated on your planet. This impression makes you sure of your destiny. Yet, you are at the brink of big upheavals that only a minority is aware of.

It is not our responsibility to modify your future without you choosing it. Consider this message as a worldwide referendum! And your answer as a ballot!

Who are we?

Neither your scientists nor your religious representatives speak unanimously about the unexplained celestial events that mankind has witnessed for thousands of years. To know the truth, one must face it without the filter of one's beliefs, however respectable they may be.

A growing number of anonymous researchers of yours are exploring new knowledge paths and are getting very close to reality. Today, your civilization is flooded with an ocean of information of which only a tiny part, the less upsetting one, is notably diffused.

What in your history seemed ridiculous or improbable has often become possible, then realized, in particular in the last fifty years. Be aware that the future will be even more surprising. You will discover the worst as well as the best.

Like billions others in this galaxy, we are conscious creatures that some name "extra-terrestrials", even though reality is subtler.

There is no fundamental difference between you and us, save for the experience of certain stages of evolution. Like in any other organized structure, hierarchy exists in our internal relationships. Ours is based upon the wisdom of several races. It is with the approval of this hierarchy that we turn to you.

Like most of you, we are in the quest of the Supreme Being. Therefore we are not gods or lesser gods but virtually your equals in the Cosmic Brotherhood.

Physically, we are somewhat different from you but for most of us humanoid-shaped.

Our existence is a reality but the majority of you does not perceive it yet. We are not mere observations, we are consciences just like you. You fail to apprehend us because we remain invisible to your senses and measure instruments most of the time.

We wish to fill this void at this moment in your history. We made this collective decision but this is not enough. We need yours. Through this message, you become the decision-makers ! You personally.

We have no human representative on Earth who could guide your decision.

Why aren't we visible?

At certain stages of evolution, cosmic "humanities" discover new forms of science beyond the apparent control of matter. Structured dematerialization and materialization are part of them. This is what your humanity has reached in a few laboratories, in close collaboration with other "extra-terrestrial" creatures at the cost of hazardous compromises that remain purposely hidden from you by some of your representatives.

Apart from the aerial or spatial objects or phenomena known about by your scientific community, that you call 'UFOs, there are essentially multidimensional manufactured spaceships that apply these capacities.

Many human beings have been in visual, auditory, tactile or psychic contact with such ships, some of which are under occult powers that "govern" you. The scarcity of your observations is due to the outstanding advantages provided by the dematerialized state of these ships.

By not witnessing them by yourself, you cannot believe in their existence. We fully understand this.

The majority of these observations are made on an individual basis so as to touch the soul and not to modify any organized system. This is deliberate from the races that surround you but for very different reasons and results.

For negative multidimensional beings that play a part in the exercise of power in the shadow of human oligarchy, discretion is motivated by their will to keep their existence and seizure unknown.

For us, discretion is motivated by the respect of the human free will that people can exercise to manage their own affairs so that they can reach technical and spiritual maturity on their own. Humankind's entrance into the family of galactic civilizations is greatly expected.

We can appear in broad daylight and help you attain this union. We haven't done it so far, as too few of you have genuinely desired it, because of ignorance, indifference or fear, and because the emergency of the situation did not justify it. Many of those who study our appearances count the lights in the night without lighting the way. Often they think in terms of objects when it is all about conscious beings.

Who are you?

You are the offspring of many traditions that throughout time have been mutually enriched by each others' contributions. The same applies to the races at the surface of the Earth. Your goal is to unite in the respect of these roots to accomplish a common project. The appearance of your cultures seems to keep you separated because you substitute it to your deeper being. Shape is now more important than the essence of your subtle nature. For the powers in place, this prevalence of the shape constitutes the ramparts against any form of jeopardy.

You are being called on to overcome shape while still respecting it for its richness and beauty. Understanding the conscience of shape makes us love men in their diversity. Peace does not mean not making war, it consists in becoming what you are in reality: a same Fraternity.

To understand this, the number of solutions within your reach are decreasing. One of them consists in contact with another race that would reflect the image of what you are in reality.

What is your situation?

Except for rare occasions, our interventions always had very little incidence on your capacity to make collective and individual decisions about your own future. This is motivated by our knowledge of your deep psychological mechanisms.

We reached the conclusion that freedom is built every day as a being becomes aware of himself and of his environment, getting progressively rid of constraints and inertias, whatever they may be. Despite the numerous, brave and willing human consciences, those inertias are artificially maintained for the profit of a growing centralizing power.

Until recently, mankind lived a satisfying control of its decisions. But it is losing more and more the control of its own fate because of the growing use of advanced technologies, which lethal consequences on the earthly and human ecosystems become irreversible. You are slowly but surely losing your extraordinary capacity to make life desirable. Your resilience will artificially decrease, independently of your own will. Such technologies exist that affect your body as well as your mind. Such plans are on their way.

This can change as long as you keep this creative power in you, even if it cohabits with the dark intentions of your potential lords. This is the reason why we remain invisible. This individual power is doomed to vanish should a collective reaction of great magnitude not happen. The period to come is that of rupture, whichever it may be.

But should you wait for the last moment to find solutions ? Should you anticipate or undergo pain?

Your history has never ceased to be marked by encounters between peoples who had to discover one another in conditions that were often conflictual. Conquests almost always happened to the detriment of others. Earth has now become a village where everyone knows everyone else but still conflicts persist and threats of all kinds get worse in duration and intensity.

Although a Human being as an individual, yet having many potential capacities, cannot exercise them with dignity. This is the case for the biggest majority of you for reasons that are essentially geopolitical.

There are several billion of you. The education of your children and your living conditions, as well as the conditions of numerous animals and much plant life are nevertheless under the thumb of a small number of your political, financial, military and religious representatives.

Your thoughts and beliefs are modeled after partisan interests to turn you into slaves while at the same time giving you the feeling that you are in total control of your destiny, which in essence is the reality.

But there is a long way between a wish and a fact when the true rules of the game at hand are unknown. This time, you are not the conqueror. Biasing information is a millenary strategy for human beings. Inducting thoughts, emotions or organisms that do not belong to you via ad hoc technologies is an even older a strategy.

Wonderful opportunities of progress stand close to big subdual and destruction threats. These dangers and opportunities exist now. However, you can only perceive what is being shown to you. The end of natural resources is programmed whereas no long-term collective project has been launched.

Ecosystem exhaustion mechanisms have exceeded irreversible limits. The scarcity of resources and their unfair distribution - resources which entry price will rise day after day - will bring about fratricide fights at a large scale, but also at the very heart of your cities and countryside.

Hatred grows bigger but so does love. That is what keeps you confident in your ability to find solutions. But the critical mass is insufficient and a sabotage work is cleverly being carried out.

Human behaviors, formed from past habits and trainings, have such an inertia that this perspective leads you to a dead end. You entrust these problems to representatives, whose conscience of common well-being slowly fades away in front of corporatist interests, with those difficulties. They are always debating on the form but rarely on the content.

Just at the moment of action, delays will accumulate to the point when you have to submit rather than choose. This is the reason why, more than ever in your history, your decisions of today will directly and significantly impact your survival of tomorrow.

What event could radically modify this inertia that is typical of any civilization ? Where will a collective and unifying awareness come from, that will stop this blind rushing ahead?

Tribes, populations and human nations have always encountered and interacted with one another. Faced with the threats weighing upon the human family, it is perhaps time that a greater interaction occurred.

A great roller wave is on the verge of emerging. It mixes very positive but also very negative aspects.

Who are the "third party"?

There are two ways to establish a cosmic contact with another civilization: via its standing representatives or directly with individuals without distinction. The first way entails fights of interests, the second way brings awareness.

The first way was chosen by a group of races motivated by keeping mankind in slavery, thereby controlling Earth resources, the gene pool and human emotional energy.

The second way was chosen by a group of races allied with the cause of the Spirit of service. We have, at our end, subscribed to this disinterested cause and introduced ourselves a few years ago to representatives of the human power who refused our outstretched hand on the pretext of incompatible interests with their strategic vision.

That is why today individuals are to make this choice by themselves without any representative interfering. What we proposed in the past to those whom we believed were in a capacity to contribute to your happiness, we propose it now to ... you!

Most of you ignore that non-human creatures took part in the exercise of those centralizing powers without them being neither suspected nor accessible to your senses. This is so true that they have almost very subtly taken control. They do not necessarily stand on your material plan, and that is precisely what could make them extremely efficient and frightening in the near future. However, be aware that a large number of your representatives are fighting this danger ! Be aware that not all abductions are made against you. It is difficult to recognize the truth !

How could you under such conditions exercise your free will when it is so much manipulated ?

What are you really free of?

Peace and reunification of your peoples would be a first step toward the harmony with civilizations other than yours.

That is precisely what those who manipulate you behind the scenes want to avoid at all cost because, by dividing, they reign! They also reign over those who govern you. Their strength comes from their capacity to distillate mistrust and fear into you. This considerably harms your very cosmic nature.

This message would be of no interest if these manipulators' tutorate did not reach its peak and if their misleading and murderous plans did not materialize in a few years from now. Their deadlines are close and mankind will undergo unprecedented torments for the next ten cycles.

To defend yourselves against this aggression that bears no face, you need at least to have enough information that leads to the solution.

As is also the case with humans, resistance exists amongst those dominant races. Here again, appearance will not be enough to tell the dominator from the ally. At your current state of psychism, it is extremely difficult for you to distinguish between them. In addition to your intuition, training will be necessary when the time has come.

Being aware of the priceless value of free will, we are inviting you to an alternative.

What can we offer ?

We can offer you a more holistic vision of the universe and of life, constructive interactions, the experience of fair and fraternal relationships, liberating technical knowledge, eradication of suffering, controlled exercise of individual powers, the access to new forms of energy and, finally, a better comprehension of consciousness.

We cannot help you overcome your individual and collective fears, or bring you laws that you would not have chosen, work on your own selves, individual and collective effort to build the world you desire, the spirit of quest to new skies.

What would we receive ?

Should you decide that such a contact takes place, we would rejoice over the safeguarding of fraternal equilibrium in this region of the universe, fruitful diplomatic exchanges, and the intense Joy of knowing that you are united to accomplish what you are capable of. The feeling of Joy is strongly sought in the universe for its energy is divine.

What is the question we ask you ?

"DO YOU WISH THAT WE SHOW UP ?"

How to can you answer this question ?

The truth of soul can be read by telepathy. You only need to clearly ask yourself this question and give your answer as clearly, on your own or in a group, as you wish. Being in the heart of a city or in the middle of a desert does not impact the efficiency of your answer, YES or NO, IMMEDIATELY AFTER ASKING THE QUESTION! Just do it as if you were speaking to yourself but thinking about the message.

This is a universal question and these mere few words, put in their context, have a powerful meaning. You should not let hesitation in the way. This is why you should calmly think about it, in all conscience. In order to perfectly associate your answer with the question, it is recommended that you answer right after another reading of this message.

Do not rush to answer. Breathe and let all the power of your own free will penetrate you. Be proud of what you are ! The problems that you may have weaken you. Forget about them for a few minutes to be yourselves. Feel the force that springs up in you. You are in control of yourselves !

A single thought, a single answer can drastically change your near future, in one way as in another.

Your individual decision of asking in your inner self that we show up on your material plan and in broad daylight is precious and essential to us.

Even though you can choose the way that best suits you, rituals are essentially useless. A sincere request made with your heart and your own will will always be perceived by those of us whom it is sent to.

In your own private polling booth of your secret will, you will determine the future.

What is the lever effect ?

This decision should be made by the greatest number among you, even though it might seem like a minority. It is recommended to spread this message, in all envisage-able fashions, in as many languages as possible, to those around you, whether or not they seem receptive to this new vision of the future.

Do it using in a humorous tone or derision if that can help you. You can even openly and publicly make fun of it if it makes you feel more comfortable but do not be indifferent for at least you will have exercised your free will.

Forget about the false prophets and the beliefs that have been transmitted to you about us. This request is one of the most intimate that can be asked to you. Making a decision by yourself, as an individual, is your right as well as your responsibility !

Passivity only leads to the absence of freedom. Similarly, indecision is never efficient. If you really want to cling to your beliefs, which is something that we understand, then say NO. If you do not know what to choose, do not say YES because of mere curiosity. This is not a show, this is real daily life, WE ARE ALIVE ! And living !

Your history has plenty of episodes when determined men and women were able to influence the thread of events in spite of their small number.

Just like a small number is enough to take temporal power on Earth and influence the future of the majority, a small number of you can radically change your fate as an answer to the impotence in face of so much inertia and hurdles ! You can ease the mankind's birth to Brotherhood.

One of your thinkers once said: "Give me a hand-hold and I'll raise the Earth".

Spreading this message will then be the hand-hold to strengthen, we will be the light-years long lever, you will be the craftsmen to ... raise the Earth as a consequence of our appearance.

What would be the consequences of a positive decision ?

For us, the immediate consequence of a collective favorable decision would be the materialization of many ships, in your sky and on Earth.

For you, the direct effect would be the rapid abandoning of many certitudes and beliefs.

A simple conclusive visual contact would have huge repercussions on your future. Much knowledge would be modified forever. The organization of your societies would be deeply upheaved for ever, in all fields of activity. Power would become individual because you would see for yourself that we are living. Concretely, you would change the scale of your values !

The most important thing for us is that humankind would form a single family in front of this "unknown" we would represent !

Danger would slowly melt away from your homes because you would indirectly force the undesirable ones, those we name the "third party", to show up and vanish. You would all bear the same name and share the same roots: Mankind !

Later on, peaceful and respectful exchanges would be thus possible if such is your wish. For now, he who is hungry cannot smile, he who is fearful cannot welcome us. We are sad to see men, women and children suffering to such a degree in their flesh and in their hearts when they bear such an inner light.

This light can be your future. Our relationships could be progressive.

Several stages of several years or decades would occur: demonstrative appearance of our ships, physical appearance beside human beings, collaboration in your technical and spiritual evolution, discovery of parts of the galaxy.

Every time, new choices would be offered to you. You would then decide by yourself to cross new stages if you think it necessary to your external and inner well-being. No interference would be decided upon unilaterally. We would leave as soon as you would collectively wish that we do.

Depending upon the speed to spread the message across the world, several weeks, or even several months will be necessary before our "great appearance", if such is the decision made by the majority of those who will have used their capacity to choose, and if this message receives the necessary support.

The main difference between your daily prayers to entities of a strictly spiritual nature and your current decision is extremely simple : we are technically equipped to materialize!

Why such a historical dilemma ?

We know that "foreigners" are considered as enemies as long as they embody the "unknown". In a first stage, the emotion that our appearance will generate will strengthen your relationships on a worldwide scale.

How could you know whether our arrival is the consequence of your collective choice ? For the simple reason that we would have otherwise been already there for a long time at your level of existence ! If we are not there yet, it is because you have not made such a decision explicitly.

Some among you might think that we would make you believe in a deliberate choice of yours so as to legitimate our arrival, though this would not be true. What interest would we have to openly offer you what you haven't got any access to yet, for the benefit of the greatest number of you ?

How could you be certain that this is not yet another subtle maneuver of the "third party" to better enslave you ? Because one always more efficiently fights something that is identified than the contrary. Isn't the terrorism that corrodes you a blatant example ?

Whatever, you are the sole judge in your own heart and soul ! Whatever your choice, it would be respectable and respected ! In the absence of human representatives who could potentially seduce into error you ignore everything about us as well as from about those who manipulate you without your consent.

In your situation, the precautionary principle that consists in not trying to discover us does no longer prevail. You are already in the Pandora's box that the "third party" has created around you. Whatever your decision may be you will have to get out of it.

In the face of such a dilemma, one ignorance against another, you need to ask your intuition. Do you want to see us with your own eyes, or simply believe what your thinkers say ? That is the real question!

After thousands of years, one day, this choice was going to be inevitable: choosing between two unknowns.

Why spread such a message among yourselves ?

Translate and spread this message widely. This action will affect your future in an irreversible and historical way at the scale of millenniums, otherwise, it will postpone a new opportunity to choose to several years later, at least one generation, if it can survive.

Not choosing, stands for undergoing other people's choice. Not informing others stands for running the risk of obtaining a result that is contrary to one's expectations. Remaining indifferent means giving up one's free will.

It is all about your future. It is all about your evolution.

It is possible that this invitation does not receive your collective assent and that, because of a lack of information, it will be disregarded. Nevertheless no individual desire goes unheeded in the universe.

Imagine our arrival tomorrow. Thousands of ships. A unique cultural shock in today's mankind's history. It will then be too late to regret about not making a choice and spreading the message because this discovery will be irreversible. We do insist that you do not rush into it, but do think about it ! And decide !

The big medias will not be necessarily interested in spreading this message. It is therefore your task, as an anonymous yet an extraordinary thinking and loving being, to transmit it.

You are still the architects of your own fate...

"DO YOU WISH THAT WE SHOW UP ?"

www.ingramcontent.com/pod-product-compliance
Lightning Source LLC
Chambersburg PA
CBHW062138280526
45788CB00001B/208